PERSPECTIVES ON WRITING
Series Editor, Susan H. McLeod

PERSPECTIVES ON WRITING
Series Editor, Susan H. McLeod

The Perspectives on Writing series addresses writing studies in a broad sense. Consistent with the wide ranging approaches characteristic of teaching and scholarship in writing across the curriculum, the series presents works that take divergent perspectives on working as a writer, teaching writing, administering writing programs, and studying writing in its various forms.

The WAC Clearinghouse and Parlor Press are collaborating so that these books will be widely available through free digital distribution and low-cost print editions. The publishers and the Series editor are teachers and researchers of writing, committed to the principle that knowledge should freely circulate. We see the opportunities that new technologies have for further democratizing knowledge. And we see that to share the power of writing is to share the means for all to articulate their needs, interest, and learning into the great experiment of literacy.

Recent Books in the Series

Steven J. Corbett, *Beyond Dichotomy: Synergizing Writing Center and Classroom Pedagogies* (2015)

Christy I. Wenger, *Yoga Minds, Writing Bodies: Contemplative Writing Pedagogy* (2015)

Tara Roeder and Roseanne Gatto (Eds.), *Critical Expressivism: Theory and Practice in the Composition Classroom* (2014)

Terry Myers Zawacki and Michelle Cox (Eds), *WAC and Second-Language Writers: Research Towards Linguistically and Culturally Inclusive Programs and Practices*, (2014)

Charles Bazerman, *A Rhetoric of Literate Action: Literate Action Volume 1* (2013)

Charles Bazerman, *A Theory of Literate Action: Literate Action Volume 2* (2013)

Katherine V. Wills and Rich Rice (Eds.), *ePortfolio Performance Support Systems: Constructing, Presenting, and Assessing Portfolios* (2013)

Mike Duncan and Star Medzerian Vanguri (Eds.), *The Centrality of Style* (2013)

Chris Thaiss, Gerd Bräuer, Paula Carlino, Lisa Ganobcsik-Williams, and Aparna Sinha (Eds.), *Writing Programs Worldwide: Profiles of Academic Writing in Many Places* (2012)

Andy Kirkpatrick and Zhichang Xu, *Chinese Rhetoric and Writing: An Introduction for Language Teachers* (2012)

BEYOND ARGUMENT: ESSAYING AS A PRACTICE OF (EX)CHANGE

Sarah Allen

The WAC Clearinghouse
wac.colostate.edu
Fort Collins, Colorado

Parlor Press
www.parlorpress.com
Anderson, South Carolina

The WAC Clearinghouse, Fort Collins, Colorado 80523-1052
Parlor Press, 3015 Brackenberry Drive, Anderson, South Carolina 29621

© 2015 by Sarah Allen. This work is licensed under a Creative Commons Attribution-NonCommercial-NoDerivatives 4.0 International.

Printed in the United States of America

Library of Congress Cataloging-in-Publication Data

Allen, Sarah, 1975-
  Beyond argument : essaying as a practice of (ex)change / Sarah Allen.
      pages cm. -- (Perspectives on writing)
  Includes bibliographical references.
    ISBN 978-1-60235-646-7 (pbk. : acid-free paper) -- ISBN 978-1-60235-650-4 (hardcover : acid-free paper)
  1. Persuasion (Rhetoric) 2. Essay--Authorship. 3. Self in literature. 4. Persona (Literature) I. Title.
  P301.5.P47A45 2015
  808.4--dc23
                              2015006892

Copyeditor: Sarah Brooks
Designer: Mike Palmquist
Series Editor: Susan H. McLeod

This book is printed on acid-free paper.

The WAC Clearinghouse supports teachers of writing across the disciplines. Hosted by Colorado State University, it brings together scholarly journals and book series as well as resources for teachers who use writing in their courses. This book is available in digital format for free download at http://wac.colostate.edu.

Parlor Press, LLC is an independent publisher of scholarly and trade titles in print and multimedia formats. This book is available in print and eBook formats from Parlor Press at http://www.parlorpress.com. For submission information or to find out about Parlor Press publications, write to Parlor Press, 3015 Brackenberry Drive, Anderson, South Carolina 29621, or email editor@parlorpress.com.

I dedicate this work to my students.

CONTENTS

Acknowledgments ix
Introduction 3
Chapter 1: Meeting the Real Self in the Essay 19
Chapter 2: Meeting the Constructed Self in the Essay 41
Chapter 3: Cultivating a Self in the Essay 59
Chapter 4: Imitation as Meditation 75
Chapter 5: Self Writing in the Classroom 91
About the Author 141
Works Cited 143

ACKNOWLEDGMENTS

I was fortunate enough to have studied with Paul Heilker at Virginia Tech and, then, with Christy Friend, John Muckelbauer, and Pat Gehrke at the University of South Carolina. I am intensely grateful to all of them for their persistent influence on my work. This manuscript, in many ways, is shaped by (and, thus, is only possible because of) their influences. Christy Friend, in particular, continues to serve as a guide and an inspiration for my work not only as a scholar, but also as an administrator and teacher.

I would also like to thank my ever patient and thoughtful colleagues at the University of Northern Colorado, who read early drafts of the manuscript and helped me to revise it with a more diverse audience in mind. Those colleagues include Tracey Sedinger, Molly Desjardins, April Miller, Joseph Chaves, and Kristin Bovaird-Abbo.

Finally, I'd like to thank Mom, Liz, and Jason for their patience, support, and grounded perspectives throughout the process of drafting and revising this manuscript. Without them, I'm not sure that I could have sustained the work beyond the first chapter.

An earlier version of Chapter 3 was published in *Rhetoric Review* in 2010 (volume 29, issue 4, pages 364-78), under the title "The Cultivated Self: Self Writing, Subjectivity, and Debate." I wish to thank the publisher, Taylor and Francis, for permission to reproduce this material. I am indebted to the reviewers and editors at WAC Clearinghouse and Parlor Press for their invaluable feedback on the manuscript and for their support of this project. I am particularly grateful to Peter Elbow, who served as one of the reviewers, for his generous responses and helpful suggestions at various stages of the project's development.

BEYOND ARGUMENT: ESSAYING AS A PRACTICE OF (EX)CHANGE

INTRODUCTION

It is no secret that the academy has become obsessed with argument, nor is it a secret that other forms of writing have been demoted to "preparatory" work—their unique strengths diminished in the face of the rigors of argument. We college writing teachers and administrators, in particular, have become so focused on argument that we have neglected or at least devalued other exercises. In most college writing curriculum, for example, any exploration is reserved almost exclusively for the preparatory work our students do (e.g., in freewriting, journaling, and class discussion) before completing the more important work of constructing an argument. Even when we talk about Writing Across the Curriculum or Writing in the Disciplines, where there are so many other options for the kinds of writing that could be valued, we writing teachers, scholars, and administrators wave the banner of "everything's an argument." This obsession with argument becomes especially problematic when examined in relation to the uses and conceptions of argument at work in forums outside of the academy.

The forms of argument that the American public typically witnesses (e.g., playing out in political arenas and in social media forums) tend to polarize participants by trapping them in a position. Perhaps, in part, this trapping happens because there is simply not enough time in these forums to fully develop a more complex or reflective position, much less to shift a position. I'm thinking of the 2008 presidential debates and of the blog posts tacked onto almost any online newspaper article that deals in a contentious topic. Time, however, cannot be the only contributing feature in this trapping. Americans' use of argument as an aggressive and competitive mode of engagement is an immeasurable factor.

Today, instead of negotiation and compromise, there are talks of secessions and the creation of new states. Both liberals and conservatives are accused of being compulsively loyal to their respective parties, of lacking critical thinking skills about "the issues." We are so divided and intractable that our government shut down in a stand-off that had reverberating, negative effects on our political and economic lives. Unsurprisingly, there is talk about the U.S. people being "ungovernable," due to our inability to negotiate and our competitive positioning. Surprisingly, though, I've seen the same kind of polarization happen among academics—the people who are supposed to be experts at productive argument (by which I think most of us mean or hope for something more like debate). Think of the ways in which we've inherited the famous Elbow-Bartholomae exchange in *College Composition and Communication* in the early 90s, for example, or of the latest conflict about writing curriculum that erupted in your department meetings.

Of course, argument is supposed to be rendered more carefully in academically-informed spaces: participants are not supposed to ignore opposing perspectives, resort to ad hominem attacks, rely on faulty logic, or use bullying tactics. We (academics) profess that we want rational arguments—arguments that are forwarded through reason, that are constituted in rational exchange and grounded in goodwill. However, they often are not, which is really no surprise, given that, as human beings, there is often so much more at stake in any argument than its rational validity.

For example, even in the decade or so that I've been a member of professional listservs, I can't recall witnessing any scholar or teacher, who was passionately for or against the incorporation of the personal essay in college writing courses, changing his/her mind due to the persuasiveness of a particularly logical argument—certainly not publicly, anyway. Perhaps for the academic, such changes are more likely to happen in private, after s/he has had some time to mull over the claims made in a listserv conversation. On the other hand, the absence of such changes in perspective/belief may be due to a formative assumption about subjectivity that drives our conception of argument and its value both inside and outside of the academy.

What if Peter Elbow decided to give up on the concept of voice and confessed it to be no-longer productive or useful? What if David Bartholomae became an Expressivist? Yet, there are many scholars—important, field-changing scholars—whose work evolves over the course of a career. Patricia Bizzell's *Academic Discourse and Critical Consciousness*, for example, can be read as a narrative of the evolution in her thinking about academic discourse and of students' (and the field's) relation to academic discourse. Theorists such as Nietzsche and Foucault famously revised their projects during their careers (e.g., Nietzsche moved away from dialectical investigations and toward genealogies; Foucault moved away from archeological investigations and toward genealogies as well). Elbow and Bartholomae, too, have revised concepts and arguments from their earlier works. I suspect, though, that as Foucault famously points out in "What is an Author," readers struggle to make sense of such rifts, such transformations in an author's work; they are quick to overlook them entirely. Instead, readers look for unity and not just in the work, across concepts and arguments, but in the identity of the author, as it is constructed in and across texts.

We professional readers, we academics, are not above the search for or assumption about unity, even though we know better, even though we have seen changes in our own work, even though we see changes (and, in fact, hope for changes) in our students' work. We look for determinism in Foucault's work, even when his later works deliberately shift away from it; we look for brutality in

Nietzsche's, even when his later works clearly revise his prior arguments. In my conversations with colleagues at national conferences, it's clear to me that, generally speaking, we expect, too, the same of ourselves: e.g., "I am a Foucauldian." Is it arrogance on our part to expect unity in the scholar? Do we somehow assume that in the moment we graduate from our respective Ph.D. programs, we should have simultaneously "arrived" at a truth, a vision, or a way of being in the world that we can spend the rest of our careers arguing from and for?

I think, rather, that we suffer from the same burdens that politicians, students, or any person participating in an exchange suffers: the expectation that we "stay true" to who we are, that we stay true to our platforms, our beliefs, our values, and our subject positions. For the academic, the platform and the subject position are almost always defined by the ever-increasing pressure to carve out a clear and definable attitude in the discipline. The more clearly and definably "you" you are, the more singular and recognizable you are to and in the field (and vice versa).

I'm not the first to point to this effort and expectation among academics to define and narrow their professional selves through their work. In "A Common Ground: The Essay in the Academy" (1989), Kurt Spellmeyer complains of the increasing specialization in the academy and its consequent "bubble"-effect, as one might call it. According to Spellmeyer, the great bane of the thrust toward ever-increasing specialization is isolation, an inability (or unwillingness) to create connections across disciplinary boundaries. Why would I examine scholarship produced in the field of history, for example, no matter how compelling and relevant, if my argument will only be deemed credible when I work with scholarship from my own field? Why would I use works by Deleuze to help me make an argument about subjectivity, when I have defined myself as a Foucauldian? I take this one step further, though, and point to the fact that this effort toward specialization, then, disables the opportunity for debate and change.

To think of this in terms of political discourse, I propose a scenario: imagine that you are sitting in a classroom with a group of students and talking about a text in which the topic of abortion comes up. Now, imagine that one speaker identifies as a democrat and another as a republican or that one speaker identifies as a feminist and another as a conservative. I'd suggest that it takes little in the way of imagining to predict the impossibility of productive exchange in this scene. Through the emphasis on specialized niches (and, thus, subject positions), agendas and interests become unproductive and isolating in any forum in which people come together to talk about disparate beliefs, ideas, and experiences.

Here's another easy (and common) example of this specialization-turned-unproductive but in the academic sphere: I am of a generation of faculty that is about fifteen years junior to the next generation in my department. When we argue about the root-problem responsible for our students' inability to transfer writing abilities and aptitudes from one course to another, I often argue that the problem is in our inconsistent pedagogies and disconnected curriculum. My senior colleagues often argue that it is in our inconsistencies in grading criteria. We have yet to be able to come to any compromise in identifying the cause of the problems we're seeing; as such, we've yet to be able to revise our work, as a department, to address that cause. I believe that our differences stem from the generational divide: each group became specialists in composition pedagogy in different eras in the field, when what it meant to be a writing teacher and specialist was decidedly different.

Whenever I find myself avoiding such departmental conversations or when I leave them feeling frustrated and depleted, I wonder: why does it feel like such "differences" function more like fundamentalism in their polarization, in the isolation and the silencing that occurs on and from both sides? Why is it that "taking a position" has become so mired, so bogged down, in individual identities and social categories (e.g., liberal vs. conservative, junior vs. senior) that we have no means to speak, to debate and explore, across their boundaries—without shouting?

Deborah Tannen has been famously writing about our "argument culture" for decades; despite her warnings and others', the field of Rhetoric and Composition emphatically embraced the mantra that "everything is an argument." No doubt, there is a certain idealizing of the Ancient world that is driving that mantra: we have hoped that if we could teach our students that claims are profuse and negotiable, if we could teach them to be aware of such claims' contexts and implications, then we could also teach them to argue responsibly and effectively, to participate in a world of their own making—one that they could revise, if they were careful and responsible enough. The hope has been that if we could do all of this, then we could help communities to negotiate effectively within and outside themselves. As some of my colleagues who are historians like to remind me, though, this is not Ancient Greece.

Despite this fact, there are those who would argue that we should not give up on trying to make negotiations, public and private debates, function more like the debates in the agora, that we (academics) just need to try harder, be smarter. There's a part of me that agrees. I think, though, that the problem isn't necessarily in argument, itself. The problem is in the modern, Western world's common conceptions of subjectivity, and argument only amplifies the worst aspects of those conceptions. Essentially, we have been trying to teach and use a method of negotiation that worked in the ancient world because there were very different subjects working in it.

Thus, as I will show throughout this project, we need not try harder in teaching argument, but we need to teach and to practice a different notion of subjectivity. We can't just talk about it (in scholarship and in our classrooms), as we have been doing since the rise of modernism, though. We need to make it, to cultivate it. To my mind, the way to cultivate it is through privileging other kinds of writing—kinds of writing in which writers would be empowered to practice different ways of engaging with ideas, with texts, with each other. At the risk of participating in an incredibly problematic binary, I consequently turn to "the opposite" of argument for an alternative: the personal essay.

This alternative is risky, as I said, because it has traditionally inhabited the position of opposite-to-the-argument in writing studies and, thus, carries with it the byproducts of opposition (e.g., irreconcilability, mutual exclusivity). I acknowledge, too, that even without the framing of the binary, the personal essay comes with another, potentially more pressing set of problems. The very problems to which I refer came into play recently in a professional listserv of which I am a member:

In the spring of 2013, there were a series of arguments on the WPA listserv centering on the values (positive and negative) of "personal writing" in college writing curriculum. Just a few of the concerns expressed about the use of personal writing were as follows: that such writing runs counter to the goals we associate with writing argument; that it allows, if not encourages, students to ignore the sociopolitical contexts of their experiences and of their interpretations of those experiences; and that it invites students to produce work that is often not "reflective" or meditative enough. On the other hand, participants also (and often in the same posts) noted many of the positive values of personal writing: that it is a space within which to explore identities (individual and collective) and that it can create empathy between individuals and groups. By far, though, the most celebrated value of personal writing was also that-which-was-found-lacking in many student works: reflection and/or meditation. To my mind, both terms, taken in their context, denote an intense interest in analysis but with the purpose of *exploring* an idea or belief. As my colleagues pointed out in the listserv discussion, though, that exploration seems to be neglected in the personal writing produced by students.

There are scholars of the personal essay, too, who argue that the personal essay is one genre of personal writing that is valuable for the reasons I list above. They also argue that its greatest value is in its openness to the exploration and cultivation of connections—e.g., among scholarly ideas and personal beliefs, among community beliefs and personal experiences, and even among academic disciplines whose discourses have become utterly and mutually exclusive. Point being, despite common complaints about personal writing produced by our students, the genre of the personal essay actually does provide a space for student writers to do something other than argue—namely, to reflect and meditate on their experiences. It allows them to do so, even, by considering the sociopolitical contexts of their experiences and of their interpretations of those experiences—scholarly, personal, or otherwise. The question, thus, emerges: why, then, is the personal essay failing to be reflective/meditative enough, when practiced by our students?

Part of the problem with the personal essay's life in the academy is, no doubt, due to the emphasis on argument that is manifest in writing curricula, as well as in informal, public, and professional conversations. Students have inherited this obsession with argument, though they are, ironically, quick to recognize the damage that arguing-to-win causes. They know that our political "debates" are flighty and impotent, save in further dividing peoples. They know that our current use of argument encourages conflict instead of helping in the effort toward resolution and progress. They know that all of this conflict and impotence makes for a world too fragmented to understand, much less to change.

In another ironic and terrible twist, though, they also don't see much value in the form of argument that we, teachers of writing, offer them. I think that even the least savvy student recognizes that the standard college English paper taught and produced in a first-year writing course, for example, wouldn't have any real persuasive power outside of that course (in fact, it doesn't have any persuasive power in the course, since papers are produced by students to demonstrate skill, not to actually persuade the reader of a position). Are we really surprised by the highly ineffectual sound-bite arguments in presidential debates and short rants in blog posts that are responding to complex, high-stakes sociopolitical issues, when the academy, itself, teaches students to produce the kind of argument that can be captured in single statement (thank you, thesis statement) and that can be mapped out through the listing of evidence, but with very little work done to explore the complexities of any particular stance (thank you, five-paragraph essay)?

As they progress through curriculum, students tell me that they are building on the formula of the thesis-driven, five-paragraph essay by learning how to better explain in an argument why they believe what they believe and, thus, why others should believe the same. Frankly, it's a weird process. It is based on a series of assumptions that make very little sense in real time, when tested out among real people (e.g., the assumption that a position is more convincing if it can be stated in a single sentence and prior to any other real discussion about the issue). Yet, my students have inherited this version of argument so well that when I ask even my sharpest and advanced undergraduate writing students what the value is in attending to "other sides" of any argument, they always explain that the greatest value is in knowing who "the enemy" is and how to bolster one's own thesis in the face of that enemy. This belief suggests two primary assumptions: 1.

that the argument equals the person (e.g., the enemy is one who argues against me), and 2. that the value of exploring the various sides of an issue is only beneficial when it helps students to better know themselves, to better know their own arguments, and to effectively win their own arguments. When I ask if there might be other pay-offs for such an exploration, I am usually met with baffled expressions and silence.

The problem with my asking my students to explore ideas in a personal essay is that I am asking for a fundamentally different mode of engagement from them—one that may seem entirely alien or, worse, valueless to them. To my mind, the feeling of the essay being alien or valueless is deeply related to (if not caused by) the fact that it doesn't permit them the stability (of belief, but also of identity) to squat firmly in a single position and to speak from and for it. That said, it's clear to me that what students want from their writing training and what we need to offer consistently and deliberately are opportunities not for further conflict, polarization, and isolation, but for connection, negotiation, and change.

There's an awful lot about the past that does not inspire nostalgia; however, there are ways of knowing that were embraced in other times that might do us some good now, if we were to reinvent them—not whole-meal but in the rhetorical sense of the word "invention." If we were to reinvent the personal essay, then through that process, we might discover a way to engage with the beliefs and markers that constitute [individual, community, institutional] identities in different, less-divisive, more-connective ways. For example, leaning heavily on what he deems to be Montaigne's project in his *Essais* (1580), Spellmeyer presents an older way of "knowing": he states, "Montaigne's real concern is not knowledge proper, but the relationship between individuals and the conventions by which their experience is defined and contained" (263), which seems to be another way of saying that Montaigne works to examine the rhetorical-ness of his [interpretation of] experiences. This seems a fruitful way of thinking about (and writing about) the modern-day self, in knowing the self; it enables opportunities for connection in that "rhetorical-ness," as I've called it.

To explain, let me offer another example: just last semester, a student asked me why he couldn't argue for a kind of "oversoul" (but without the baggage of Transcendentalism) by using the existence of ghosts to support his argument. In speaking with this student, I found myself in a position where I had to explain what kinds of evidence count in academic argument, what kinds don't, and why—a largely rhetorical exercise. The rhetorical-ness of the exercise, in turn, makes me wonder why I cannot open up a space (in an assignment, perhaps) where such evidence could be remade as material for an exploration of this different conception of an oversoul. The personal essay would be one such space. In it, "evidence" would be transformed into objects of meditation, and as such, this student would have a chance not simply to forward a belief through a thesis that would inevitably speak most effectively and persuasively to those with a similar belief system. Instead, the objects of meditation (e.g., the concept of and belief in ghosts) would become fodder for an exploration of what counts as evidence in such a belief system and/or what the existence of ghosts might mean for conceptions of life, death, the human relationship to the natural world, etc. Those objects of meditation might, that is to say, become part of a thought experiment, one rendered in words on a page.

The value of writing in order to test an idea could be that such exercises would prove to be more important to "real world" work than even argument is. In such an approach to writing, students would have the opportunity to try out an idea, instead of having to invent an argument that, essentially, is not being used for and would not be effective in its purpose (to influence an audience). Given this practice of "trying out" an idea, instead of arguing for a claim's "rightness" and for its adoption by an audience, students might learn a different mode of engagement—one that actually enables negotiation and change.[1]

I think we all know that talking in academic argument about how to approach differences among individuals and communities, for example, is not at all like negotiating differences among individuals and communities in any other public. As one of my prior students once passionately confessed in class, "I've read all this material about Latino identities and about the oppression that occurs through our school's silencing of everything but Standard English. I get it, and I think that oppression is wrong. But, I still get really pissed off when I go to Wal-Mart and find a bunch of Latino men ogling me and making me feel like a piece of meat. How am I supposed to feel?" To which I have to say, I can't remember reading a piece of scholarship that even peripherally examines those feelings—positive or negative. To my mind, this is a serious failing on our part, as scholars and teachers; if we can't help our students connect and carry that negotiation into the world, into their lives outside of the classroom, and make it productive, then what, exactly, are we doing?

More to my point here, wouldn't the personal essay provide the answer to this gap and the others I've written of above? Couldn't it enable a different kind (a decidedly civic kind) of engagement, by bringing all of the academic work we do in our classrooms and curriculum into relationship with our and our students' very real, very personal experiences? Couldn't the personal essay provide students with an opportunity to create connections among the seemingly contradictory forms of evidence found in popular culture and in academia, as well as among the seemingly exclusive forms of knowledge found in different disciplines? Perhaps most importantly, couldn't the personal essay repair the schisms that occur between people because of the social categories and rigid beliefs that make up our subject positions?

Of course, this opportunity, if personal essay advocates were to embrace it, will require of us quite a lot of work. To begin with, there is the common complaint that the personal essay is not generally understood (across courses, across disciplines, even among essay teachers and scholars) according to any particular theory—a complaint/selling point which, at first, may seem liberating, but actually has crippling consequences.[2] For example, Wendy Bishop points out repeatedly in "Suddenly Sexy" that we, quite simply, don't know what creative nonfiction is (and thus, what the personal essay is). All we know for sure is that it can be a wonder-full, empowering form or that it can be responsible for unreflective, solipsistic, "confessional" ranting. Yet, as Bishop will go on to explain, there are qualities worth celebrating in the genre (e.g., exploration), and for those qualities, she argues for the teaching of creative nonfiction in composition classes.

I find this seeming contradiction about the genre possessing qualities/conventions but no recognized theory to be interesting and for a variety of reasons. For example, I think that the contradiction, in part, is responsible for the misconceptions and misuses of the personal essay in our writing classes. As the last "free form," the essay resists being disciplined into a theory, yet there are conventions of the essay (e.g., the use of personal voice) for which it is celebrated and persists in the academy. This project, if nothing else, constitutes several attempts at theorizing the personal essay and, at the same time, at investigating the costs and benefits of theorizing the personal essay in the different ways treated in each chapter.

More specifically, in Chapter 1, I explore the most common conception of the relation between the essayist and the essay: that the two are in a transparent relationship to one another. This conception of the essay is enabled and perpetuated through what I will argue are the three major conventions of the genre: freedom, walking, and voice. I focus the last half of the chapter on the third convention, which seems to be the most celebrated of the three because there is the most at stake in it—namely, the opportunity for empowerment through writing.

To do this work on the third convention, I turn to Expressivist notions of voice-in-writing and examine the ways in which voice is thought to manifest and operate on the page. To explore said Expressivist notions, I have taken up the work of Peter Elbow, who is generally understood by the field of Rhetoric and Composition to be the figurehead of Expressivism. As such, he seems an easy choice for my work in Chapter 1. On the other hand, as I'll discuss briefly in Chapter 1, Elbow's concept of voice is slippery. His descriptions of it are often tentative, highly metaphorical, and they evolve in important ways over the course of his career. It has been no easy task to try to pin down the concept in his work. Consequently, I rely on key passages in his work and explore them at length but always within the framework of this project's question: what might a productive theory of the personal essay look like?

In the end, I find that the voice-informed conception of the relationship between the writer and the page ultimately fails essayists who are interested in the free form of the essay and in the possibility it is supposed to engender: writing that expresses the natural or essential self, unmediated and uninhibited by social impositions. The problem is that the concept of voice in writing hinges on the assumption that a writer can transcend not only the social influences working on him/her, but also his/her own self in order to express the self in unmediated form on the page. As I will show, even if one could transcend social influences and one's own self, that transcendence would cause the self-on-the-page to function not as a subject wielding social forces but as an object acted on by the writer and the reader, one that is essentially made impotent by its pretended dislocation from "the social."

I turn, in Chapter 2, to the most popular conception of the relation between writer and page in rhetoric and composition scholarship, a conception that takes the shape of the "socially constructed" self. Bringing, again, the two disciplines of Creative Nonfiction and Rhetoric and Composition into conversation with one another, I present this conceptualization of the writer-page relation and apply it to the essayist-essay relation in order to test out a different theoretical framework for the essay. Specifically, I examine David Bartholomae's and others' work on discourse communities, Pratt's work on contact zones, and Fish's and Bizzell's work on (anti)foundationalism. I find that however much said scholars labor to move away from the problems that occur in Expressivist notions of the writer-page relation, any theory of the socially constructed self still works by objectifying the subject through the use of an impossible transcendent move. I show how this problem occurs in personal essays that enact a contact zone on the page (e.g., in essays by Molly Ivins and Linda Brodkey). In the end, I find that such essayists and scholars who are invested in the concept of a social self and its construction are still participating in what Bizzell and Fish call "theory hope" (the belief that we can transcend our socialness in order to have some say in it, in order to wield it, even), and as the same scholars so famously point out, theory hope is really just a grand pretend; it doesn't accomplish the kind of empowerment-through-engagement that it hopes.

Consequently, I find that these two potential theories of the essay don't actually accomplish what they set out to do; they don't empower the essayist to negotiate his/her self in relation to the world in the ways they promise. As much as I value both potential theories of the essay for their reflective ways of accounting for the self of the essayist and the self-on-the-page, I find myself turning to "The" great obstacle to the personal essay to find another possibility: poststructuralist theory. Many scholars of the essay emphatically proclaim that the essay is not only atheoretical but that it is opposed to poststructuralist theory.[3] For example, in his well-known article "The Essay: Hearsay Evidence and Second-Class Citizenship," Chris Anderson argues that in the essay "a certain number of a priori assumptions are allowed." He describes those assumptions as such: "the stones we kick are here, people are born, there are origins." These assumptions, he pits against "contemporary scholarship," which he describes as "articles necessitated by poststructuralism," i.e., articles "in which no assumptions about words can be taken for granted" (301).

Above, Anderson leverages what seems a common critique of poststructuralism: that in poststructuralism there are no origins, that objects don't exist, and that meaning is impossible or, perhaps, naïve. Of course, all of the criticisms listed in the above statement would present major obstacles for the essay, for the essay is celebrated for its origination in the individual essayist, is valuable precisely because reality exists and can be explored in an essay, and is at its core an exercise in meaning-making. I would argue, though, that many advocates of the personal essay, who posit it against poststructuralism, are essentially doing what the academy has done to the personal essay: misreading it. Anderson's reading of poststructuralism, for example, is misleading—at least with regard to one "poststructuralist," Michel Foucault. Though his work would easily fit into the "poststructuralist" category, in Foucault's work there are, in fact, origins, objects, and meaning, but the difference is that they are not metaphysical origins, objects, and meanings. Origins happen within a complex of relations of power, so that origins are more like junctures than sources.

In "Foucault Revolutionizes History," Paul Veyne best explains this concept of origins in response to Foucault's study of madness. He states,

> To say that madness does not exist is not to claim that madmen are victims of prejudice, nor is it to deny such an assertion, for that matter.... It means that at a level other than that of consciousness a certain practice is necessary for there even to be an object such as 'the madman' to be judged to the best of one's knowledge and belief, or for society to be able to 'drive someone mad.' (169)

To clarify, Foucault never says that madness does not exist; rather, his point, as I think Veyne is trying to explain it, is that madness does not *pre-exist* as a stable entity/category that then acts on or determines an individual's mode of existence. Instead, Foucault emphasizes that there are ways of talking (discourses) about an individual and ways of acting (practices) on/by an individual that "objectivize" (make into a subject) him/her as "the madperson." I will explore this idea at greater lengths in the third chapter.

It's important to clarify here, though, that Foucault does not mean to make "discourse" or "practices" the origin of all things either. Veyne states, "Foucault has not discovered a previously unknown new agency, called practice" (Veyne 156). Instead, these practices are "what people do," and they originate "from historical changes, quite simply, from the countless transformations of historical reality" (156). In other words, practices originate in other practices, in relation to other practices, in particular historical moments, in relation to other historical moments, at points of rupture and continuity.

Perhaps this seems a strange example, but I'm reminded of the new interest in natural horsemanship (I live in Colorado and ride a horse, so this is a discourse to which I'm privy). Many critics of the movement argue that there is nothing new in the practices of natural horsemanship; rather, they are old practices that have been repackaged in a leftist belief about how human beings should interact with animals. If so, then in this example, the practices of natural horsemanship originate in much older practices, but they have been made new in the discourse which has emerged around a responsibility to animals and to the natural world.

Of course, Foucault's conception of origins would disrupt the traditional conception of an essay's origin: that it derives from some unique essential or social makeup of the essayist. And much of poststructuralist theory would do the same, though by different means. Thus, poststructuralist theory, though it has reinvigorated the academic article in new ways, presents the essay with a supposed impasse. The problem is that when this impasse is endorsed in order to keep essay writing from adapting to different and new conceptions of subjectivity, then the genre, itself, consequently gets left behind. Indeed, one might easily conclude that the fact that the essay remains an outdated and under-theorized form is precisely why it is an often neglected form. If it can't accommodate new and different conceptions of self—especially given that it is the form that claims to be most interested in the self—then it inevitably will be discarded and replaced with modes of writing that can.

Perhaps more importantly, though, given the particular sociopolitical context within which we now work (with all of its attendant investments in argument), personal essay scholars' rejection of a more fluid, complex, "postmodern" notion of self deprives the genre of its greatest (or at least most timely) potential: to enable the productive exchange and exploration of ideas and beliefs that have constituted a momentarily fixed self. That productive exchange and exploration can disrupt the fixed self, remake it, or at least remind it that it does not have to sit, squarely, in its socially-sanctioned sociopolitical space.

I will show that there is much that at least one thought historian's "poststructuralist" theory provides in the way of a compelling and progressive study of subjectivity in essays. This is not to say that the other versions of subjectivity should be tossed out entirely. Rather, my goal (like Foucault's) is "to make visible a bygone way of approaching the self and others which might suggest possibilities for the present" (Rabinow xxvii), a way which is described in Foucault's work on the writers of Antiquity and their emphasis on the care of the self.

To make visible this other way of approaching subjectivity, in the third chapter, I turn to Foucault's work on self writing and to Montaigne's *Essais* in which I find a version of subjectivity that does not essentialize the subject. Instead, the subject is that which is constituted in the practices of the care of the self, including practices such as the truth test. Through these practices, the writer disciplines a self by enacting a relationship of oneself to oneself: the writer, the self-on-the-page, and the various practices of writing and reading all work in a complex of relations in which each subject is constituted in relation to the others. Via this conceptualization of the subject, I discover a mode of engagement that enables productive debate, a mode of engagement that isn't about argument but is about exploring ideas, a mode of engagement in which writers take seriously the texts of others, of themselves, and are *effected* by their engagement with them.

To further explore what this different mode of engagement might look like, the fourth chapter takes one kind of meditative practice in self writing and examines it much more closely. Specifically, I argue that imitation is one kind of meditative practice in which the writer must attend closely to the texts of others, test the truths available in those texts, and ultimately be re-constituted in that negotiation. As many rhetoric and composition scholars have pointed out (e.g., Connors and Corbett), imitation may work in a variety of ways: paraphrase, translation, straight copying, etc. In this chapter, I focus on how the practices of imitation can be transformed and made productive according to the ethic of the care of the self: how they encourage attentiveness, make genuine response possible, enable change or transformation, etc. To do so, I examine the ways in which Seneca, Foucault, and Nietzsche make use of the same metaphor (the beehive), referencing each other's use of the metaphor explicitly, but then constituting the metaphor differently within their own work and, thus, transforming the metaphor, their work, and the self-page relation. One of the most exciting implications of this examination of imitation as a practice in the care of the self is that, despite concerns about assimilation and homogeneity in imitation, the possibilities for the constituting of the subject and for self-transformation seem limited only by the variety and complexities of the truths and contexts that are available to writers for imitation.

That said, I anticipate that essay teachers might still be tempted to slip back into a belief about writers being capable of transcending the practices of the care of the self, of transcending the texts writers imitate and/or produce, of transcending even one's own constituting. So, for the final chapter, I will share course assignments, student writings, and reflections for a course in self writing. After all, this belief in transcendence is pervasive. For many of us, it was part of our training. ("Teach students to see how they are made by societal norms, and they can refuse that making.") In particular, I will provide writing assignments and readings which can help students negotiate in and among (often contentious) discourses. If students come to see this negotiation as one that occurs among discourses (instead of among distinct and essentialized individuals/communities), then that negotiation—with all of its attendant practices (e.g., analysis and revision)—will not be simply another instance of foundationalism. Rather, negotiation among discourses necessitates awareness that knowledge itself is constituted in those discourses, not prior to them, and that the subject that emerges in response to said negotiation is not some unique combination of the essential characteristics of particular cultures or of the writer's mind or soul, but is, itself, constituted in those discourses and by that negotiation.

My hope is that essay teachers and scholars, as well as writing curriculum administrators, will begin to see the value, again, of the personal essay and that they will remember its rigorousness, when they see the genre's potential as it is enabled through the practices of the care of the self. I hope that essayists and essay scholars and teachers will find themselves less afraid, if they were to begin with, of "theory" and that they will feel encouraged to further explore potential theories of the essay so that it can take its proper place in the academy as a rigorous and explorative form. Most importantly, I hope that essayists (student and professional) will hear my call to use the essay as a space for the cultivation of a very different kind of subject, one that is capable of producing, living in, and negotiating connections—across our disciplines, as well as across our communities and selves. We advocates of connection, we practitioners of it, will have to find ways of coming together, of working together, and the essay is one remarkable way of doing so.

NOTES

1. In this emphasis on a different mode of engagement, we too, as academics, would be contributing to change (in the academy, in the world, in our students, in ourselves). Perhaps, then, we wouldn't be complacent in what Patricia Bizzell calls "the anti-intellectualism of the American academic." She explains this anti-intellectualism as "[the American academic's] reluctance to emerge from our respective disciplines, to act as intellectuals in the larger community of the whole university and the whole society" ("Foundationalism and Anti-foundationalism" 220).

2. Of course, there are theories of the essay. In fact, I'll refer to many of the works that theorize the essay in Chapter 1; however, my point is that there is no particular theory of the essay that essay scholars acknowledge as grounding the discourse.

3. Notably, the loudest complaint by essay scholars against "poststructuralism" is specifically directed at Derrida's critique of the logocentric conception of presence—the assumption that words make present the thing to which they refer (for example, the words of an essay make present the essayist). Unfortunately, as a result, the baby has been tossed out with the bathwater, as the saying goes. In other words, the assumption seems to be that if Derrida's "poststructuralist" theory defies the work that essays are supposed to do—e.g., to work within "the realm of 'human evidence'" (Anderson 301)—then essay scholars shouldn't take up poststructuralist theory at all in order to study essays and essay writing.

To offer another example of essay scholars' resistance to poststructuralist theory, I point to Graham Good's study of the essay, *Observing the Self: Rediscovering the Essay*. In it, he states:

> Montaigne and Bacon would also undoubtedly have rejected Derrida's textualism as scholastic, as privileging the order of words over the order of things. It was exactly against that mentality that the essay originally reacted. But academia, with its concern to organize discourse into disciplines, will always tend to give priority to 'theory,' to the structures of learning; the unstructured, or rather, personally and provisionally structured, world of the essay is all the more necessary as a counterweight. (182)

This is an explicit and typical example of the leap that is often made in essay scholarship, a leap from a resistance to Derrida's work to a refusal of "theory" all together. This seems to me a dangerous and debilitating leap because, in this case, it dismisses other provocative and productive possibilities.

CHAPTER 1: MEETING THE REAL SELF IN THE ESSAY

> Knowing that Nature never did betray
> The heart that loved her; 'tis her privilege,
> Through all the years of this our life, to lead
> From joy to joy: for she can so inform
> The mind that is within us, so impress
> With quietness and beauty, and so feed
> With lofty thoughts, that neither evil tongues,
> Rash judgments, nor the sneers of selfish men,
> Nor greetings where no kindness is, nor all
> The dreary intercourse of daily life
> Shall e'er prevail against us, or disturb
> Our cheerful faith, that all which we behold
> Is full of blessings. Therefore let the moon
> Shine on thee in thy solitary walk.
>
> —William Wordsworth

The essay is habitually talked about in terms of its relationship to its writer. Teachers of the essay, for instance, often tell students that the essay is a space for self-discovery and for self-exploration. For example, in "Suddenly Sexy," Wendy Bishop argues that this is at least one major reason why composition teachers should incorporate creative nonfiction (the umbrella genre under which the personal essay is now housed) into their classrooms. This incorporation, she believes, would help "encourage students *to meet themselves in their writing*" (273, emphasis added). In the creative nonfiction courses that I've taught for more than a decade, I find that writing students, in turn, are consistently enthused about writing essays for precisely this possibility. In particular, they appreciate having the opportunity to practice using the conventions of the genre that are supposed to enable the possibility of meeting themselves in writing: the use of the first-person singular in such a way that the "I" refers specifically to them (not to a fictive or constructed narrator); and the use of their own experiences to explore a topic that is personally meaningful to and chosen by them. If they use these conventions effectively, then they consequently should find out more about who they are, as they discover what they think, believe, and feel in the processes of essaying and of examining the shaping text.

On the one hand, I must admit that it is very likely that my students are enthusiastic about the self-focused requirements of the essay simply because of the course's place within our curriculum. In other words, many students have confessed to me that they like the genre because by the time they take the course, they are so used to writing arguments and literary analyses, they are excited to write something, anything, new. On the other hand, as Lynn Z. Bloom argues in "Living to Tell the Tale," their enthusiasm could also be attributed to the fact that people want to talk about themselves—about who they are, what they think, what they feel, and what experiences they've had. As one of my prior students aptly put it, "Everybody's most interested in her own self because it's through the 'I' that we live."

I believe, though, that the appeal of the personal essay may also and, perhaps, primarily be due to its celebration of a simpler notion of the self and that self's relation to the world—a notion that is not as complicated as our postmodern conceptions of the self, of reality, and of the relations between them. These postmodern notions of the self, we are intimately aware of, if we work in the humanities. They inevitably inform how we teach literature and writing. These "postmodern notions" are, in fact, part of the very atmosphere of the academy. I'm thinking, for example, of Lester Faigley's decisive work, *Fragments of Rationality: Postmodernity and the Subject of Composition* (1992), in which Faigley considers, at great length, the fragmentary, the contradictory, and the consuming subject; I'm thinking, too, of Susan Miller's *Rescuing the Subject* (1989) in which Miller theorizes the postmodern subject as one who "both originates with, and results from, a written text" (15).

Today, it seems that discussion about the postmodern subject has focused its attention onto, and its tenor in response to, what we might call the materialistic and narcissistic subject (e.g., I'm thinking of the agonized and/or frustrated reflections I see weekly in professional listserves on the changing student demographic—a demographic accused of being more interested in making money and having fun, in their iPhones and Instagram accounts, in selfies and statuses, than in an education that gets them the academy's promised pay-off of social consciousness and cultural critique). No doubt, this is part of the reason behind writing teachers' suspicions about the genre of the personal essay: they worry that it not only perpetuates an overly simplistic concept of the subject but that, in so doing, the genre also risks encouraging the consumer-mentality and narcissism so many educators find at least disconcerting, if not deplorable, in today's college students. To put it simply, if students believe who they are is equal to what they like and buy, then the essay may become little more than an exercise in affirming that belief.

To be clear, I believe that these suspicions or worries about the essay are born of the assumption that the essay is necessarily a space into which the subjectivity of the writer—the real-world referent of the text's "I"—is expressed and examined. According to this assumption, the essay serves as one space where writers can take a long, hard look at *how* they look, how they see themselves and the world: through what narratives, what tendencies, what beliefs, what values, what experiences. In short, it is in the essay that one can see clearly his/her own subjectivity. However, the whole exercise stops at looking/seeing. There is nothing in the conventions of the personal essay that requires anything more than that. There's nothing in them that requires students to challenge (or change) what and/or how they see.

In sum, assumptions about the genre and, in particular, about the writer-page relation in the genre can prove problematic. Consequently, this chapter examines the more generic conception of the relation between the writer and the page in the personal essay. To get at that relation, I examine three major conventions of the genre: freedom, walking, and voice, which circulate in examples of scholarship about the genre. In examining these three conventions, I find that they enable and, in turn, are enabled by a particular conception of subjectivity. In this mutually enabling relation, I find a compelling, seductive, but also contradictory and intensely problematic theory of the personal essay.

A significant portion of this examination will focus on one of the three conventions—voice. Voice in writing is a concept that most writing teachers are familiar with, and most would acknowledge that the concept seems to be rooted in a romantic notion of the writer-page relationship. Though such a relationship between the flesh-and-blood writer and the textual self may seem antiquated, if not downright dangerous, to many of us teaching writing in the academy, that conception of the relationship has not gone away, and in fact, it still holds powerful sway over writers and readers of essays—practitioners, scholars, teachers, and students alike. Too, it is still powerfully present in Rhetoric and Composition, no matter how much we think we've moved on to the interest/bent we like to call "social constructionism." In fact, because of their mutual interest in voice, essayists and voice-invested compositionists explain the relationship between the writer and his/her text in significantly similar ways. To trace that similarity and use it to conduct a textured analysis of voice, the last half of this chapter will move away from essayists' articulations of that relationship and focus at length on compositionists' articulations of the processes of "meeting the self in writing."

Chapter One

FREEDOM

Of the primary convention of the essay, voice, essayist Scott Russell Sanders states in "The Singular First Person":

> We make assumptions about that speaking voice [in an essay], assumptions we cannot make about the narrators in fiction. Only a sophomore is permitted to ask if Huckleberry Finn ever had any children; but even literary sophisticates wonder in print about Thoreau's love life, Montaigne's domestic arrangements, De Quincey's opium habit, Virginia Woolf's depression. (194)

I point to this quote to demonstrate that there is a problem with the premise driving common conceptions of the relation between essay and essayist that I'll trace out here. The problem is that in order for Sanders's argument to work, first one must buy the premise that the essay is the expression of the writer's self. Only then would one be permitted to ask questions about the essayist, like those listed by Sanders. As to where that premise might come from, I will speculate a bit below, but for now, it's worth noting that said premise would not even be possible without the first convention of the genre: freedom. As essay scholar Michael Hall says in "The Emergence of the Essay and the Idea of Discovery," the personal essay is free from "the constraints of established authority and traditional rhetorical forms" (78), e.g., the constraints of a whole literary tradition that the writer must speak to and within. As such, it can be and do other things. It can be, for example, the embodiment of the essayist.

Of course, the interesting irony here is that there are, in fact, conventions of the essay—qualities that make an essay recognizable as such. The most important of those conventions is also the one that is most inherently contradictory: the essay's freedom from the conventions of a literary tradition. The essay is not supposed to be about conventions, about the great essayists, the great literary movements, and the great sociopolitical concerns that came before (or that emerged during) the essayist's foray into essaying. Rather, the essay is a form without tradition. To explain, in another ironic move (ironic because it argues for the essay's freedom from tradition by historizing it), Michael Hall argues that the essay came about in response to the huge shifts in thinking that emerged just prior to and during the Renaissance—shifts that emphasized and celebrated the exploration of unconstrained possibilities.

Freedom is important to the work of the essay because it makes possible something other than participation in the confining conventions of a literary tradition. Instead, according to Sanders, "an essay is [...] about the way a mind moves, the links and leaps and jigs of thought" (192). He goes on to explain that in this movement, the mind (which he equates to a dog hunting in "the underbrush of thought") "scatters a bunch of rabbits that go bounding off in all directions." The essayist must then chase a few of these metaphorical rabbits and avoid "plodding along in a straight line" (192). This requirement of chasing the jigging and jagging lines of thought is bound up in what Sanders argues, after Emerson, is the essayist's job: to "fasten words again to visible things" (Emerson 88 and Sanders 191), including, it seems, the essay to the essayist, or more specifically, the essay to the essayist's mind.[4]

Essayists working from this premise take their cue from a conception of a mind-essence relation that is more than 2000 years old (or at least, they take it from a particular reading of that conception). In Georg Lukács's influential chapter on the essay in *Soul and Form*, he points out that in a free form (the essay), "an intellect … believes itself to be sovereign" (2). Without constraints, without the parameters imposed by a more rigid genre, the mind does as it will. In that freedom, it is likely to work according to its own tendencies, its own habits, according to its own logic. And if it is working according to its own tendencies, habits, and logic, then it is free to see the writer's essential, unmediated self (what Lukács refers to as the "soul").

To explain this, Lukács invokes Plato's argument that "only the soul's guide, the mind, can behold it" (5).[5] To clarify this relation between the mind and soul a bit further, I point to the supposition here that not only are the mind and soul separate, but that the mind's purpose is to know and to guide the soul. What's interesting in this articulation of purpose is that while one could easily reason that in this statement, Plato is actually arguing that "the *rational* mind" should rein in the impulses of the more passionate (and impulsive) parts of the self, essayists use the claim to argue that where the mind is freed from any obligation to the boundaries of convention, the soul is better or more truthfully revealed. To explain this through Sanders's metaphor, if the essayist's mind is like a hunting dog chasing thoughts, then the key to the essay is in granting that mind plenty of freedom to chase whatever thoughts it likes wherever it likes. What will emerge in the course of this run over open land, so to speak, is a soul that is finally free to emerge as it truly is—without the constraints of social mores, without the expectations imposed on us according to our gender, ethnicity, class, etc., and without, it seems, even the confines of rationality (a socially-sanctioned way of thinking).

WALKING

Perhaps it is unsurprising, then, to find that the next major convention of the essay concerns the chase itself—i.e., how one chases what thoughts one wants to

Chapter One

chase and, consequently, reveals the unmediated, unconstrained self. That *how* is understood as being like a journey into nature, which traditionally involves a long, meandering, contemplative walk in the woods.[6] In short, the walk in nature serves as a metaphor for essaying, and there's a long tradition of essayists using this metaphor in their essays to reveal both the nature of the essay and the nature of the essayist's self. Essayists typically describe the self-realizing/self-remembering process that they underwent in their latest visit to the woods (or to the mountains or to some other remote expanse of nature); in turn, via the description of the distillation of the natural self, the essay comes to embody that self.[7]

For example, in the anthologized essay, "An Entrance to the Woods," Wendell Berry explicitly invokes the metaphor of walking and simultaneously enacts that movement on the page. He writes of walking through the woods and shedding "all the superfluities" of his life. For Berry, this shedding or "stripping," as he calls it, is made possible only in "the absence of human society." He states, "The necessities of foot travel in this steep country have stripped away all superfluities. I simply could not enter into this place and assume its quiet with all the belongings of a family man, property holder, etc. For the time, I am reduced to my irreducible self" (677). By walking through the woods without the cumbers of all his worldly obligations and through the subsequent effects of that walking (i.e., the quieting and the reducing of the obligations of the worldly self), Berry discovers his natural self, what he calls his "irreducible self."

This discovery happens not only in the process of walking-in-the-woods but in the process of walking-on-the-page, and Berry points to this play. Note the tense he uses as he states, "Slowly my mind and my nerves have slowed to a walk. The quiet of the woods has ceased to be something that I observe; now it is something that I am a part of" (678). He writes as though he is walking in the woods at this moment. And, he notes that by walking in nature (and now in the essay), he no longer simply observes the quiet of the woods; he becomes a part of it. I would suggest, then, that for Berry, discovering the irreducible self involves a return to what he is a part of naturally—nature—while moving away from what is not "natural"—society. This movement, he does not simply describe but enacts in the essay, not only because of the verb tense he uses, but because the essay lingers in and wanders through the issue [of discovering his natural/irreducible self]. The return to the natural self via the movement of the essay seems most important to the work of the essay because through this return, the natural self—the self that is buried/diluted when integrated with society—emerges.

In another famous example of discovering the natural self through the freeing experience of walking in nature, William Hazlitt is able to shed the superfluities or "impediments," as he calls them, of life in his essay, "On Going a Journey."

Hazlitt states, "The soul of a journey is liberty, perfect liberty, to think, feel, do, just as one pleases. We go a journey chiefly to be free of all impediments and of all inconveniences; to leave ourselves behind, much more to get rid of others" (181). Again, Hazlitt is freed in journeying, not only in the described real-world journey, but in the journey enacted in the essay, because the essay provides him with the singularly unimpeded and open space that he only otherwise finds in walking/journeying alone in nature. He states, "I want to see my vague notions float like the down of the thistle before the breeze, and not to have them entangled in the briars and thorns of controversy. For once, I like to have it all my own way; and this is impossible unless you are alone [...]" (182). Similar to Sanders's metaphor of a dog chasing rabbits, Hazlitt is describing the meandering, seemingly haphazard movement of his mind ("my vague notions float like the down of the thistle before the breeze"), freed from social constraint/obligation ("not to have them entangled in the briars and thorns of controversy"), bound only by his own desires/impulses ("all my own way").

Of course, Hazlitt, too, says above that he is freed in journeying of even his self ("leav[ing] ourselves behind"). The self that Hazlitt writes of leaving, though, is apparently the impeded and burdened self, for as he journeys, he discovers another self: "Then long forgotten things, like 'sunken wrack and sumless treasures,' burst upon my eager sight, and I begin to feel, think, and *be myself* again" (182, emphasis added). Again, the natural self seems to be capable of being discovered in the shedding of our social-ness, in a journey into what is natural.

The appeal of this simpler notion of the self and of the self's relation to the world, perhaps, is obvious. It offers us the possibility of getting away from the world, getting away, even, from our worldly selves. Our students certainly see the appeal. I'm reminded of at least a few of my students' essays in which they have written about a nostalgia for a more natural self, which equals, for them, a simpler mode of being—e.g., a self that has to worry about tilling the land or making bread for the family dinner, instead of a self that has to worry about paying bills and submitting papers and negotiating the competing versions of self that are maintained at the job, in the classroom, on Facebook, and at the dinner table. I'm reminded, though, too of many of the same student essays in which they experience some paralyzing moment in which they are confronted by a storm or a rattlesnake or a twisted ankle, while walking in the woods. In those moments, they realize that people built what we know to be "modern life" (of self-satisfaction and convenience) for many good reasons: to stave off threats and fears, to make surviving easier, but also so that we can concentrate on other stuff (like how best to treat a horse, how best to educate citizens, how best to negotiate the animosity between warring factions of people).

Sure, taking a walk can be relaxing; even commercials are now advising us to do so. But, my student essayists, even when waxing poetic about the benefits of getting away from it all, always, eventually realize that the effort doesn't actually get us away from our (postmodern) selves. Perhaps this example will do more to reveal my own fears than to prove my point, but I offer this personal example of my own daily walks: there are moments when I find that the rhythm of my own feet and the playful present-ness of my dog's experience of various spots of grass and of the other animals we meet along the way inspire a kind of dumb but also hyper-sensory state in me; however, I never get to stay in that state long. I am constantly jarred back into a much more "postmodern" reality with all of its splintering and spreading power dynamics: by men honking their horns as they pass us, by my comparison of my own body to the bodies of the women we pass at the pool, by the apparent economic differences between the lives lived in the neighborhoods we pass, by the tensions expressed in the "vote for" signs nailed to the yards we pass, and so on.

There is simply no simpler self, not without that simpler self being made in a grand pretend. Even the moments I mention above in which I describe myself as dumb and hypersensitive are not, to my mind, indicators of my having discovered a simpler self. Rather, I suspect that they are simply moments when I am given over to the present and have stopped worrying; they are not the momentary revelations of a distilled me. That said, none of this awareness, in my own or in my students' meanderings in nature and/or on the page, of the essay's failure to really capture a simpler self through the first two conventions of freedom and walking diminishes the essay's valuing of or value granted by voice.

VOICE

The two concepts—voice and walking—are pointing to intimately related processes: the first points to *the power* of the movement of a mind on the page (I'm invoking terms from Peter Elbow's work here, which I'll explore at greater lengths in the coming pages); the latter points to, describes, the movement itself, as I've discussed above. I find, however, in my readings about essays that the concept of voice has emerged as the convention that readers (and presumably, writers) care most about in the genre.[8] For example, Scott Russell Sanders states, "The essay is a haven for the private, idiosyncratic voice [...]" (190). This assumption about the genre being conducive to the writer's voice is so ingrained in essays and essay scholarship that voice seems an inescapable or inevitable part of the genre. For example, in their Introduction to one of the most widely used essay textbooks *The Fourth Genre,* Robert Root and Michael Steinberg state, "[...W]e are aware of [essayists'] presence, because their voice is personal, individual [...]" (xxiv). Again, this statement suggests that voice in an essay is a given ("we are aware")—but also that it is proof of the essayist's presence on the page.

In his extensive study of George Eliot's writing voice over the course of her literary life,[9] Robert Strange frames much of his study around the assumption that the narrator in her works is the "figure which George Eliot has animated with her own convictions and made to speak with the clarity and authority of her own celebrated authority" (326). It should come as no surprise that Strange can assert that "this figure" re-presents Eliot's own convictions and speaks with her own authority, given that the text is an essay (specifically, a "moral essay"). Because of the common conception of the essayist-essay relation I've been describing, Strange can assert that even through the fictional character in a moral essay, the writer speaks and is manifest. It is through the writer's "authorial voice," in particular, that Strange hears the writer in her essays.

In the conventions of freedom, walking, and voice, the assumption is that there is a direct and transparent relationship between the essayist and the essay; in fact, I have often found that this relationship is the ultimate goal, if not the driving force, for writing or teaching the essay. According to voice scholars in Composition Studies, though, it is not through walking [in nature and/or on the page] or even in the freedom of the form that one finds voice; rather, it is through a series of operations—e.g., reflection and speaking/breathing—which can be enacted in a personal essay to create voice in writing.

Reflection

In his article addressing the distinction between tone and voice, Taylor Stoehr states, "Voice is the pervasive *reflection*, in written or spoken language, of an author's character [...]" (150, emphasis added). Like the image we see in the mirror, voice must be a copy of the real face, or in this case, the real writer's character.[10] Stoehr continues: "There are as many possible voices as there are tones of voice, but a writer has only one voice, and while he may modulate it with many tonalities, it remains his idiosyncratic way of talking" (150). To extend the metaphor of the mirror, then, the image may reflect the apparent changes of the real face—the changes brought on by age, sleep, hairstyle, makeup, and so on—but the image remains, even in all these changes, the unique reflection of the person.

In his Introduction to *Landmark Essays: On Voice and Writing*, Peter Elbow is a bit more careful about asserting that voice is equal to the writer's self; however, he admits that he "tend[s] to lean toward" (xxviii) the view that "people do have some kind of identity that exists apart from the language they use, and that it's worth trying to talk about whether or not that identity shows in a textual voice" (xvii). Given his career-long investment in the conceptualizations and pedagogies of voice and given the field of Rhetoric and Composition's general understanding of his role as one of the central figures of the Expressivist movement, perhaps it's no surprise that I read Elbow's work as consistently asserting that something of the writer can and should necessarily show up in the voice on the page. As to what the "something" is, though, that's one of the major questions that drives much of his work, and there's no easy way to pin down what that something is.

In investigating the writer-page relation, Elbow draws, in part, on discussions of ethos in order to demonstrate that there is a very old and established tradition that takes seriously the fact "that listeners and readers get a sense of the real speaker and his or her virtue (or the absence of it) through the words on the page" (xvii).[11] According to Elbow's argument, the success of a piece is in large part determined by the personality of the writer finding its way onto the page (or into the speech) and, then, into the reader's experience of that page. Consequently, in Stoehr's and Elbow's work on voice in writing, there is at least one common thread—the assumption that language can be used as a medium for capturing some essential part of the writer's self on the page.

If we follow this assumption and apply it to the essay, then it seems easy enough to conclude that in the essay, the mind has a unique opportunity, due to the openness of the form, to take advantage of this conception of language. Imagine: there are no constraints in the form, and the language, itself (the tool for expression), is a veritable reflecting pool.[12] There are at least a few operations that have to be working in order for the process to unfold, though, which I will trace out through an extended engagement with Peter Elbow's work. Those operations include the following: the writer would have to reflect an essential part of his/her self into language, and the language would have to reflect back to the reader not just an image of the writer's self, but some real, meaningful, powerful part of the writer's self. To begin then, these operations lie in a very old theory of language.

SPEAKING IN WRITING: A THEORY OF LANGUAGE

After giving an example of a "jargony piece of educational writing," Elbow states, "[The writer] must have had a sense of the intended meaning and then *constructed* words to express it. The words lack breath or presence. [...It] would take her an extra step of revising—and revising consciously for the sake of voice—to change her written words so as to break out of that *language-construction* into a *saying-of-words* on paper" (*Writing With Power* 288-289, emphasis in text). In sharing this quote with a few of my literature colleagues and my rhetoric colleagues, the response to it is consistent: it usually ranges from raised eyebrows to an audible "grrr." When I share the same quote with my Creative Writing colleagues, the response is also consistent, but differently so: it usually ranges from a nod of the head to an audible, "duh!" This difference is interesting. It suggests that what is a given in one sphere is not in another, even though we all teach the same students from the same curriculum in the same department. To my mind, it is The fundamental difference between creative writing teachers' and scholars' conceptions of the writer-page relationship and literature teachers' and scholars' conceptions of the writer-page relationship. The source of that difference seems to be rooted in two different conceptions of language.

Expressivists, by definition, work from a philosophy of language that privileges the speaking subject, much like what I have found in the work of the French philosopher, Georges Gusdorf. In his work, Gusdorf is interested in the relationship between the writer and the text; he's especially interested in that relationship with regards to creative nonfiction (e.g., autobiographical) texts, which is why I bring him into this discussion. His most famous and extensive study of that relationship is rendered in *La Parole*, which is a phenomenological philosophy of language that, to my mind, captures in readable and useful ways a logocentric theory of language (one that is reminiscent of the object of much of Jacques Derrida's criticism).

In "Scripture of the Self: 'Prologue in Heaven,'" Gusdorf argues that speech "is what constitutes the real and what founds identity" (113). He continues, saying that speech "initiate[s] being" (113). In the context of his larger work, I understand this claim to mean that speaking has the power to create a living, breathing entity, and that in the process of speaking, one can shape that being into an identity… but not just any identity. According to Gusdorf, the initiated being is an extension of the living, coherent, original speaker. This extension is possible because, according to Gusdorf, written or spoken language is consciousness, itself—"inner speech" made external, "expos[ing] the innermost human recesses to inspection and judgment" (113).

In Gusdorf's model, after speaking, writing becomes "a second incarnation…" of the utterance of the speaker. He states, "[Writing] is the memory and the commemoration of spoken utterances, which thus will be able to confront the very one who, having spoken them, might very well have forgotten them" (114). So, in writing, the writer has the opportunity to study a finite form of the initiated being—which, in the case of creative nonfiction, is his/her self. To put this in phenomenological terms, in writing autobiographically, one discovers the self by making an observable object of it, but an object that is an extension of the original self. The key pay-off for Gusdorf in such a writing exercise is that it is only through the work of autobiography, in which he includes the essay (127), that we are able to search out our true selves, not in comparison to an other that is not us (like Adam does with Eve) but according to an other that is us.

This objectification of the self onto the page (the making of the flesh-and-blood writer into an "I" or "me" on the page) is important, key in fact, to the concept of voice. It is also responsible, as I will show in the coming pages, for voice's failure to do what it is supposed to do—to express and empower the self of the writer. To explain how voice is supposed to empower writers, I turn now to some of Peter Elbow's work on voice. In it, Elbow relies on a theory of language similar to Gusdorf's (though he does not map it out explicitly, like Gusdorf does), and it is through that theory of language that Elbow argues that by writing—by making our inner speech (i.e., life force) external—we externalize the self. If this externalization is done adequately in writing, then the externalization is of the writer's life source, which Elbow calls "*resonant* voice."

Elbow states that resonant voice consists of words that "seem to *resonate with* or *have behind*" them the unconscious as well as conscious" writer's mind. As a result, the reader feels "a sense of presence with the writer" ("About Voice" xxxiv, emphasis in text), and that is where its power lies. Elbow is careful in his phrasing here. He says "a sense of presence," as if to suggest that the experience is sensory, not necessarily scientific—i.e., predictable, objective, the inevitable consequence of a cause-effect relation. This carefulness in phrasing, tentativeness even, is typical of Elbow's work on voice. It suggests that he is experimenting with the concept, that he is testing out an idea, practicing, perhaps, the very practices he teaches in his writing textbooks (e.g., the believing/doubting game). I note this in order to clarify the fact that Elbow's investigations into and experiments with the concept of voice have yet to come to an end. He continually revises them. Thus, his work makes for a difficult object of study, as the object, itself, is often shifting and is still being revised. In this part of his ever-evolving exploration of voice, however, in the claim about words seeming "to resonate with or have behind them the unconscious as well as conscious" writer's mind, one finds, again and obviously, an emphasis on the writer's mind somehow being captured and made present in the text.[13]

This emphasis is interesting to the effort in this chapter to investigate the relation between the personal essay and the concept of voice in writing because it demonstrates the sometimes obvious (but often complicated) relationship between the ways in which one Expressivist, Peter Elbow, is emphasizing the writer's mind-page relation and the ways in which personal essayists, too, have emphasized the same relation. In Elbow's work and in the arguments about personal essays, this essential part of the writer (his/her mind) may be made present like an image in a mirror or made present in the aural qualities (the resonance) of the text, but the important point here is that the presenting of the mind on the page should be powerful enough that it impacts the reader: s/he sees it, feels it, and is affected by it, when s/he reads. To encourage that impact, Elbow advises writers to make careful choices about what kind of language they use. This advice is meant to help the student express the "invisible self"—a deeper self that exists behind or hidden within the apparent self, one that is full of power, that can extend itself beyond the physical boundaries of the flesh-and-blood writer, that can manifest in, for example, black squiggles on white pages. This self is, if framed in the discourse of and about the personal essay, the natural state of being that is so essential to the relationship between essayist and essay on which this chapter centers.

RESONANT VOICE: WHAT IT IS AND WHAT IT IS NOT

In *Writing With Power*, Elbow states, "[Some people's] speech sounds wooden, dead, fake. Some people who have sold their soul to a bureaucracy come to talk this way. Some people speak without voice who have immersed themselves in a life-long effort to think logically or scientifically [...]. Some people lack voice in their speech who are simply very frightened [...] " (290). Here, voice is somehow bound to a person's essence, his/her soul, for in the lines above, it is in selling his/her "soul to bureaucracy" that one might find oneself without a voice. That is, though, only one example of lost voice. The voiceless might be, instead of soul-selling bureaucrats, logically or scientifically-minded. The afraid may also find themselves voiceless.[14] According to this passage, then, it is bureaucracy, logic, science, and/or fear that may steal (or to which one relinquishes) a writer's voice.

In opposition to this theft or sacrifice, Elbow states, "Writing with voice is writing *into which someone has breathed*" and "[w]riting with real voice has the power to make you pay attention and understand—the words go deep." He continues, "I want to say that it has *nothing* to do with the words on the page, only with the relationship of the words to the writer—and therefore that the same words could have real voice when written by one person and lack it when written by someone else" (299, emphasis added). In other words, the power of a text hinges on the proximity of the relationship between writer and page, and Elbow takes this relationship very seriously, suggesting a proximity that is similar to the magical acts described in the Old Testament.

To explain, if one takes seriously Gusdorf's assertion that language is "not simply designation, but an immanent reality by virtue of which it is possible for man to repeat the denominative and at the same time creative act of God" (*Speaking* 12), then one sees how voice works as a divine act. The "first word" of God works like a text that has voice and vice versa. The speaker/writer is able to call into being a self, his/her self, the same self or part of the same self that exists outside of words into words. Adam is created "in the image of God"… "from the word of God." In the voice on the page one finds a reflection of the creator, the writer, but most importantly to my point here, one that is alive; some essential, life-giving, life-sustaining force remains.

Following this lineage and applying it to prior discussions about freedom and walking (the return to nature) in the essay, for voice to be breathed into the words on the page and for it to call into being the self that is the writer, the voice and its source must be in its natural state. They cannot be contaminated, diluted, or deadened by bureaucracy, logic, science, or fear. These are important requirements, for it seems that what is driving them is the assumption that such influences impede the expression of the natural (and the most potent) self. If the natural self is impeded, then the power of voice fails, for in voice theory, words not only issue from my essence, but generate power in issuing from and carrying the force of that essence.

According to Elbow, there is evidence of that power in the writer's words, if they impact the reader's center. He states, "[…T]he words somehow issue from the writer's center—even if in a slippery way—and produce resonance which gets the words more powerfully to a reader's center" (*Writing With Power* 298). To enact resonant voice, then, the words of a text should "somehow issue from the writer's center," from his/her essence, resonating powerfully enough to effect a thrust into "the reader's center."

As to what that center is, it's difficult to say. Elbow certainly does not explain explicitly what it is, though he does seem to oscillate in terminology between the writer's "mind" and the writer's "center." If there is a commonality between the two, it is in the assumption that both are the *inside* of a person. The interiority is the writer's clunky violin or chest cavity (two metaphors Elbow uses at length to explain voice), the place from which s/he can speak his/her self. And in that speaking [of] self, [of] his/her innerness, s/he will assume the creative power of something like a god—the capacity to call his/her self into being. The stakes, for Elbow, are these: real voice is what he hopes to teach his students in order to empower them, for if I see what I am inside—beyond social influences, "impediments," or obligations—I can use this essence as the space from which to say "no" to those social impositions.

Empowerment in Voice

Within this assumption that voice grants us a space from which to say "no," voice becomes the means to liberation. Gordon Rohmann and Albert Wlecke state, "[By] merely permitting students to echo the categories of their culture, they would never discover themselves within the writing process" (7). This is the most common argument for voice—and the rally-cry that has met with the most backlash from composition scholars. Here is the crux of the voice issue: an emphasis on voice is opposed to an emphasis on "the categories of [our] culture." Voice is invested in who I am essentially, which is necessarily and significantly opposed to who I am socially. To put this in other terms, the thinking around the value of voice in writing (that it liberates) generally goes something like this: my essence is innate, and it is the key to my individuality, to my uniqueness. In a culture that privileges the autonomy of the individual, my uniqueness, and its expression, is not simply innate, but is, in fact, my birthright.

This thinking is rooted in an ideology that is, arguably, the nucleus of Western notions of subjectivity. In this emphasis on the individual and his/her unique essence, social forces or categories are believed to be necessarily working on us to oppress us, to silence our innerness and its potential expression. For Elbow, these social forces may be the socially privileged influences called "bureaucracy" or "science." For Stoehr, they might be the conventions of literature at a given moment in history. For bell hooks, one of the most celebrated and renowned advocates of voice, they might include racism and sexism.

In hooks's work, the stakes of voice-in-writing are best demonstrated: it is against the formidable foe of racism that she speaks. In speaking against racism by voicing her self, hooks argues that she moves from object-position (object of racism) to subject-position, to a position of autonomy where she is able to say "no" to racism. hooks states,

> [C]oming to voice is an act of resistance. Speaking becomes both a way to engage in active self-transformation and a rite of passage where one moves from being object to being subject. Only as subjects can we speak. As objects we remain voiceless—our beings defined and interpreted by others. That way of speaking is characterized by opposition, by resistance. It demands that paradigms shift—that we learn to talk—to listen—to hear in a new way. (53)

The presupposition is that when we don't speak as individuals, as subjects, we let our selves be defined and interpreted by others, according to assumed social categories (like race, gender, social class, etc). So, for example, in hooks's experience as a student in a writing class, where "the teacher and fellow students would praise [her] for using [her] 'true,' authentic voice" when she wrote a poem in "the particular dialect of Southern black speech," she felt this praise "mask[ed] racial biases about what [her] authentic voice would or should be" (52). She insists that writers must, instead, write in the voice that can combat stereotypes and racial biases, a voice that she explains as "liberatory voice—that way of speaking that is no longer determined by one's status as object—as oppressed being" (23). Herein lies the interesting hypocrisy of voice: hooks's concept of voice is about making the writer a subject, not an object, but for me to reflect or resonate or "express" my distinctive self, the self must be objectified in the re-presentation on the page. It becomes that-which-is-outside, that-which-is-there; it becomes that-which-is-me (an object).

This theory of voice, of the self-page relation, hinges on the older, magical theory of language that I articulated earlier, one in which language functions as a vehicle that, basically, carries the essence of an entity. As a result, the self on the page can be pointed to and designated by an object pronoun, such as "me" or "her," but because that reflection is of myself, it can also be designated by a possessive pronoun, such as "my" or "her" ("that is my self, my voice on the page"). In such ways, the self-on-the-page is both separate from the writer and intimately related to it. It is made separate from the writer, in part, out of necessity: if, according to Berry or Hazlitt, one must isolate the self from society, from social influence—making it an entity separate from the social forces that act on/in it—then that self-on-the-page must be separated, even, from the actual self that is the flesh-and-blood writer; it must be separated from all of the impositions on the writer, and it must be purified, distilled in that separating. Yet, even in that separation, the self-on-the-page is still deeply related to the writer—thus the possessive relationship ("that is my voice"), indicating a kind of pointing simultaneously inward and outward to name the relationship, to claim the self-on-the-page.

I acknowledge that this 'me'-on-the-page can influence the reader—and thus, function *like* an agent. But, if the liberatory voice, if the resonant voice, in this conception of subjectivity, is supposed to possess the life force of the writer and is supposed to be an agent (which here equals the slayer of social forces, the shedder of social impositions), then of course, the self-on-the-page fails. It fails because it *is* language, made of language, possible only as language, which is a decidedly "social" phenomenon. Language is its own imposition—giving shape to an experience by giving experience a name, a category ("that is a tree" or "this is love"), a shape that only makes sense in relation to other names, other categories ("it is like a bush but taller" or "it is an affection but more than that"). Montaigne offers one of the best examples of the social phenomenon of language in "Of Experience." He states, "I ask what is 'nature,' 'pleasure,' 'circle,' 'substitution.' The question is one of words, and is answered the same way. 'A stone is a body.' But if you pressed on: 'And what is a body?'—'Substance'—'And what is substance?' and so on, you would finally drive the respondent to the end of the lexicon" (818-819). Language refers to itself; it is, it functions via, relations between and among words, which explain concepts, not the "thing in itself."

Language is not the vehicle for the life force of a living being. Despite any romantic notions about the writer's relationship to the page, we know that words do not carry the writer's mind or soul (if they did, conversations about the value, preservation, and destruction of texts would be very different). Rather, language can only constitute a textual self, one that is then imposed upon when it is read by others—even by the writer.

WHERE VOICE FAILS, WHY IT REMAINS, AND WHERE TO NEXT

Of course, as I've demonstrated in this chapter, this concept of voice in writing does not acknowledge the social theory of language I describe above. Yet, hooks recognizes that voice in writing is always a social act, a political act, that it cannot be isolated from context. Elbow, too, begins his first major book, *Writing Without Teachers*, with this statement: "Many people are now trying to become less helpless, both personally and politically: trying to claim more control over their own lives. One of the ways people lack control over their lives is through lacking control over words" (vii). He acknowledges here that writing is both a personal and political act. Too, if we push our students just a little on this point about language and about the writer-page relation, they, too, see the problems. I've yet to meet a student essayist who has been able to describe his/her self in asocial or pre-social ways, e.g., according to qualities other than his/her class, religious affiliation, political beliefs, etc. Who am I, if not my age, gender, education, ethnicity? Who am I without my relationships to others, as a colleague, sister, teacher, or friend? And, perhaps even more importantly, how can I talk about myself without a culturally, historically, politically-bound language—without using the syntax and vocabulary made available to me by the society I speak within and to?

Too, though "write your true self" might be a call that (re)invests student writers in the work of the writing classroom and (re)invigorates their relationships to their own texts—which, in turn, can (re)make me, as teacher, into an inspiring figure—I, for one, feel very uncomfortable with the requirement that I, then, grade my students' selves-on-the-page. But, all of these points have been made by others, throughout the last few decades, as the Humanities has turned its attention to "the social" (I'll take up this turn at length in Chapter 2). So, why does this particular conception of subjectivity hold such sway over essayists, student essayists, essay scholars, and essay teachers, alike?

Many writers and scholars want to and do buy into a belief in a self untouched by "the social," a self that is pre-social and that they can access through particular practices. Many of the essayists and scholars discussed here work from the assumption that in a more integral self, a different truth—a truer truth—

can be found. This truer truth, if it issues from that essential part of the self, is more powerful. It can make change, influence others, and ultimately, stop the damning social influences that work to bury it. This, I suspect, is why many of my colleagues who are for or against the teaching of the personal essay in our curriculum are quick to point out that one of the benefits and drawbacks (again, depending on if one is for or against the essay) is that these "truer truths" are often those that are felt, that are unprovable, and that in privileging such truths in the essay, those truths can be expressed and, thus, can become part of the discourse (e.g., think of the example of the student who wanted to write about ghosts, which I talk about in the Introduction). The problem, of course, is that such truths, when understood as issuing from the essence of the writer, become undebatable truths; they cannot be proven, cannot be refuted, cannot be analyzed and critiqued beyond their own givens. And, therein lies the danger.

At one time, I, too, wanted access to and permission to express some pre-social self—and all the truths that felt right. But in so doing, as I'll show in the next chapter, I had enabled a classroom that could only perform at an expressive level, that could not engage beyond solipsistic discovery. This process can be, no doubt, valuable to us and to our students. However, the process cannot stop there, if said truths are going to get any traction in the discourses in which we work and/or want to participate.

In conclusion, for all its virtues in encouraging students to write and in helping composition and essay scholars to articulate the relationship between the writer and the self-on-the-page, voice theory doesn't allow me to voice my center, my innerness without making an object (something exterior) of it—an object that is, ironically, made of the social stuff of language. I encounter this self, this voice, through the operation of objectification, where the self-on-the-page is not my mind, but an object rendered in language that is perceptible by my mind. The most damning problem, though, is that in that move to objectify my mind by expressing it on the page, I do not negotiate with the social and overcome it; rather, I [pretend to] avoid "the social," altogether—which, to be frank, can only make me impotent, even irrelevant, in relation to it.

These failings of voice theory have expansive implications. For example, if the writer is not writing and the reader is not reading the essayist's self, as subject, on the page, as is so often assumed, then what is being written/read? If the essay is not the writer's manifested mind on the page, then how does one argue for any interesting relationship between writer and page? Can one derive the latter's meaning in relation to the former (or vice versa)? The questions proliferate, as do their consequences. Perhaps, the most important question is this: If I can't discover and express my self through voice in an essay in order to know my natural self and to resist the oppressive forces working to manipulate me, then by what other means can I know my self, if at all, and negotiate with or resist those forces in writing? To come at this question and a few of the earlier questions from another angle, this project turns now to the other side of the debate over subjectivity in writing—the social.

NOTES

4. It's important to note, at the beginning of this exploration, that essayists tend to differ about what kind or aspects of self one might meet on the page. However differently essayists might describe the particulars of what they see on the page, though, they generally agree that one can see the writer's self on the page through the conventions of the personal essay.

5. In the *Phaedrus*, Plato calls the mind "the pilot of the soul" (52).

6. Undoubtedly, walking-as-essaying is an old and persistent analogy. According to Paul Heilker in his landmark text, *The Essay: Theory and Pedagogy for an Active Form*, the analogy has its roots in the "consistent and unbroken line of agreement about the nature and form of the essay running from its originators to contemporary essayists and theorists: the essay is kineticism incarnate—the embodiment of perpetual mobility, motion, and movement" (169). For example, in a study on the essay as a reflective text, Réda Bensmaïa states that the essay is "an efficacious means to realize and implement the mind's 'mobility'" (xxxi). Thus, the essayist does not simply describe the walking mind, but the essay, itself, is walking because it is a fluid, moving form.

As Paul Heilker examines much more extensively in *The Essay*, there are many images used to describe the movement of the essay: flying, slithering, flowing, journeying, walking, rambling, wandering, meandering, roaming, exploring, searching, seeking, venturing, following, tracking, and hunting. These images, he groups together in some cases, but notes that they constitute "an extended family of tropes which relies, at its core, upon a conflation of physical, mental, and textual journeying" (173). Heilker continues, "Upon this notion of the essay as journeying is built a branching family of closely related images, the most elementary of which is the image of essay, essay writing, and essay reading as walking" (174). Again, "walking" is not simply an image or a trope for what the essay looks like, but is a description of the essay as "kineticism incarnate."

7. It should be noted that part of the appeal of the "walking" metaphor is that it is vague. As I've explained in the section in this chapter titled "Freedom," the essay is supposed to be unstructured. Heilker builds on this idea that the essay is unstructured in the traditional sense (e.g., like a scholarly argument) but argues that it is still organized, that it still has "form." Specifically, he argues that the essay is organized "chrono-logically," which is a term he uses to describe a kind of kairos-driven orga-

Chapter One

nization of thought, where in the process of writing, the writer responds to what s/he is writing. As such, the text moves in an unstructured but organized way.

8. No doubt, this is because of the long and passionate practice (by rhetoric and composition scholars and essayists, alike) of polarizing the essay and the argument as irreconcilable opposites with the one championing personal voice and the latter championing scholarly authority. See William Gass's "Emerson and the Essay" for a particularly powerful example of this polarization from a writer who is both an essayist and scholar.

9. This kind of work—extensive studies of particular writers' voices—is done much more often in literary criticism than in composition scholarship. This is one of the critiques in current discussions of voice in the field of Composition Studies—that voice-invested scholarship has not done enough work to apply a theory of voice to particular texts (see, for example, Elbow's relatively recent *College English* article, "Voice in Writing Again: Embracing Contraries").

10. In voice scholarship, there is rarely a distinction made between "author" and "writer"—a point that Harris makes in his treatment of Elbow's work in his chapter on voice in *A Teaching Subject*. There is a difference, however, when the two concepts are considered through the lens of Foucault's work. For Foucault and in most poststructuralist theory and scholarship, the author is but a conception of the writer. It is based on what is known of the writer through his/her written texts, and this knowledge is social, contextual; it circulates in a culture and informs the ways in which a text circulates. The writer is something else. It is, too, a concept, but it refers to the one who writes, not the figure in whose conception we can (or, according to Barthes, should not) read a text.

More to the point here, in Stoehr's work there seems to be no distinction between author and writer. I use his choice of word in this section in order to avoid any confusion created by my using a different term.

11. "Virtue," as the key ingredient in effective ethos, comes to us from the works of classical rhetors (e.g., Aristotle). Elbow is drawing on this tradition.

12. Of course, since Nietzsche first wrote "On Truth and Lies in a Nonmoral Sense" (in 1873), if not since the sophists (see Susan Jarratt's *Rereading the Sophists*), the transparency of language has been called into question. Nietzsche famously explains in "Truth and Lies" that language always operates as metaphor, that it cannot capture "the thing in itself," so to speak, that it is an arbitrary designation for some piece of reality—e.g., the designation of T-R-E-E for the reality of the tree—and that, really, we are only getting access to the human conception of that piece of reality when we invoke the [relative] word. Thus, in order to buy this argument about the transparency of language, one must first buy into a much older theory of language—one that is intensely problematic for granting language a power that I can only describe as "magical."

13. There are ways in which Elbow's work has been inherited by the field as utterly and perfectly Expressivist in nature, when in truth, it is not necessarily so—a terrible consequence, perhaps, of the "author function," as Foucault explains it. Much of my reading of his work is informed and therefore limited, inevitably, by that inheritance.

14. Stoehr argues that these influences—of fear or uncertainty, namely—are "failures of tone" (150). In his model, tone is "an author's attitude toward his audience," which he argues is different from "an author's character." The difference in each scholar's assessment of what one calls "failure of tone" and the other "voicelessness" seems to be the result of what are different projects: Elbow is interested in voice-as-empowerment; Stoehr is interested in distinguishing between tone and voice.

CHAPTER 2: MEETING THE CONSTRUCTED SELF IN THE ESSAY

> I'm no heroine
> I still answer to the other half of the race
> I don't fool myself
> like I fool you
> I don't have the power
> You know, we just don't run this place
>
> - Ani Difranco, "I'm No Heroine"

Last spring, I had a student who jeered at the rape and murder of women in the personal essays he submitted to me and to the class. When I first met with the student to talk about the content in his essays, he was hostile: "But this is who I really am!" he exclaimed. "I have a twisted sense of humor!" At the time of our conference, we were reading works by Peter Elbow and bell hooks on voice, and in response to those works, he felt empowered to tell the truth, his truth, on the page. To be frank, this was a revelatory moment for me as a writing teacher; I realized that the concept (the convention in essay writing) that I had practically come to worship over the years because I and my students had found it to be so inspiring had provided this student with fodder for a terrible expression. By invoking the concept of voice, this student was indeed justified in voicing, through the expression of his truth, what he saw as his true self, even if that voicing silenced, marginalized, or threatened others.

The problems with this concept of voice in the personal essay have major implications. As explained through the examples of Berry's and Hazlitt's essays in Chapter 1, one such implication is that the social world's influence functions primarily as a threat to the essayist's true self and, as such, is an influence to be rejected. To put this in my student's perspective, he felt that in a truly authentic personal essay, he should discard what he considered to be "prudish ideas about sex," imposed on him by a society that did not allow him to be and express who he really was. In this example, the principal trap of voice emerges clearly: voice in the essay works by privileging one voice, the individual writer's voice, over all others. Thus, if one were to take seriously the idea that one can and should voice his/her soul or mind in an essay, then voicing that soul or mind necessarily becomes an act of domination, where the writer's voice silences other voices in order to make itself heard. Consequently, despite its work to subvert any social act of domination, "voice" only perpetuates it—by establishing its own.

This is what I call an "it's-all-about-me ethic," by which I am referring to the essayist's obligation to what Didion famously calls the writer's "implacable 'I.'" As Lynn Z. Bloom explains, "Writers of creative nonfiction live—and die—by a single ethical standard, to render faithfully, as Joan Didion says in 'On Keeping a Notebook,' *'how it felt to me'* (134), their understanding of both the literal and larger Truth. That standard, and that alone, is the writer's ethic of creative nonfiction" ("Living to Tell the Tale" 278, emphasis added). The ethical imperative of the essayist is to be true to his/her interpretation of what is happening in and around him/her. The writer owes nothing else to the reader, not even consideration of the social implications of the truth that the writer feels/interprets. Given this ethic, this responsibility, it is no wonder that the personal essay has its critics.

VOICING MY SELF V. CRITIQUING CULTURE

There are many rhetoric and composition scholars, perhaps the most famous and persuasive of which is David Bartholomae, who argue that writing teachers are not doing their students any favors by privileging the often unreflective personal narratives that commonly constitute students' personal essays. Specifically, Bartholomae argues that creative nonfiction students write "[...] as though they were not the products of their time, politics and culture, as though they could be free, elegant, smart, independent, the owners of all that they saw" ("Writing" 70). Despite the unsettling suggestion that student writers are only imagining themselves as "elegant [and] smart," [15] Bartholomae's argument has gotten a lot of traction among writing teachers; many, today, would agree with his claim that in creative nonfiction (including personal essays), students write without considering sociopolitical influences on their identities.[16] To put this in other terms, writing teachers often complain that students write personal essays as if they (the student and the essay, itself) are not what many in the field of Rhetoric and Composition call "socially constructed."

For Bartholomae, this shortcoming in creative nonfiction is due to the fact that through their encounters with the genre, students are not taught how to participate responsibly in any given discourse community; instead, in creative nonfiction, they are asked to state what they already know of their own experiences and selves. As such, like a subject caught in "the matrix" and unaware of his/her own entrapment, more often than not, students' essays reflect the very hegemony that may be oppressing them, precisely because voice privileges "telling my story" for what it means to me over "examining my story" for how it participates in a larger discourse. Essentially, the line drawn in the sand here is between the two very different practices of self-expression and social critique.

This difference in practices is essential. Writing teachers and essay teachers, in particular, generally sympathize with Bartholomae's call for 'examination' over 'telling' in personal essays; however, the same teachers would see his insistence that the practice of examination function more like critique as one that flies in the face of Elbow's or any other voice-advocate's call to voice the self in writing. In fact, in other works, most famously in *Writing Without Teachers*, Elbow argues that the role of the reader-as-critic (including the writer-as-reader-as-critic) is counterproductive to expression, even to thoughtful or reflective expression, inhibiting it like any social influence would.[17] Of course, it is in response to this claim that Bartholomae leverages his own argument in "Writing with Teachers: A Conversation with Peter Elbow," which I quote above and which is the first piece of the famous debate between the two scholars in *College Composition and Communication* (Feb. 1995)—a debate that in some ways marks the separation of Creative Writing's and Rhetoric and Composition's treatment and valuing of the genre of the personal essay.[18]

VOICE AND THE SOCIAL SELF

At least in the field of Rhetoric and Composition, it would seem that in response to the debate between Peter Elbow and David Bartholomae about whether composition teachers should emphasize voice or participation in discourse communities (i.e., scholarly critique) in their writing courses, rhetoric and composition scholars and teachers have responded by doing a bit of both—by still calling the subject-on-the-page the "voice" of the writer and by still arguing that the voice is created and owned by the writer. Now, however, the field generally acknowledges that any voice on the page comes from and is created according to the writer's "situatedness." For example, in *Voicing Ourselves*, Christian Knoeller states, "Thus, the field [of Rhetoric and Composition] has moved beyond accounts of 'authentic' voice as individual identity, to situate voice within discourse communities: a means for signaling membership and establishing authority" (9). In another example, one voice scholar, Lizbeth Bryant states, "A writer constructs a voice out of his or her social milieu: a constructed subject voice that correlates with the writer's position in his or her world" (6). Point being, the *en vogue* theory of voice in the field of Rhetoric and Composition is one which figures the subject-on-the-page as possible not through the expression of the mind/soul of the writer, but through the construction of the writer's identity—which the writer specifically and deliberately constructs by "participating in" particular social contexts.

This conception of voice has found its way into essay scholarship, as well, though it hasn't gotten the same traction.[19] For example, essayist Douglas Atkins argues that the writer must select, "like selecting an article of clothing," his/her voice within each context. He argues that the voice of the writer must be "real": "[meaning] truthful within the created context" (170). In taking seriously the analogy of picking out an article of clothing to wear, readers can infer that by "real" Atkins is referring, more specifically, to a voice that functions, as a concept, more like ethos but with a strong, necessary, and explicit tie to the personality and [socio-historico-political] circumstances of the real writer. Still, as I demonstrated in Chapter 1, the more common conception of the essay is that it is deeply wedded to some essential part of the self, a self that is imposed upon by the social world and that is best realized by being brought into an intentional relationship with the natural world. There is not much discussion, by comparison, of a concept of voice in personal essays that adheres to this idea of the socially constructed self.

On the other hand, I think I state the obvious when I point out that in the field of Rhetoric and Composition, there is a massive amount of scholarship available on the socially constructed self in writing; the concept is so pervasive that it has become invisible, even, in its inscriptions on the field. Consequently, in this chapter, I will introduce and explore the tenets of the field's conception of the socially constructed self in order to give it shape and make it perceptible. I will bring that conception into relation with, and apply it to, a few personal essays in order to explore how this different conception of voice might function in the personal essay. Thus, this chapter is a kind of thought experiment, one I attempt for a few reasons: to explore this other option for how we might understand the relation between the writer and the page in an essay; to discover how this option is meant to free the essayist (or writer, more generally) from some of the traps of the conception of voice discussed at the beginning of this chapter and in Chapter 1; and, finally, to demonstrate that because of the operations of objectification and transcendence that are foundational to this conceptualization of the writer-page relationship, it functions in much the same ways as the prior conception, creating similar traps and others of its own for the essayist.

WRITING ESSAYS [BY] PARTICIPATING IN DISCOURSE COMMUNITIES

The terms sometimes shift, but the basic tenets of any conception of a socially constructed self and its voice(s)-on-the-page are consistent: 1) the voice-on-the-page or the "textual self," as I'll call it in this chapter, is constructed by the writer, who is a participant in various "discourse communities"; 2) conventions and practices of the various discourse communities in which one participates more than likely come into conflict with each other; and 3) the conventions and practices of any discourse community, as well as any internal and external conflicts in and among them, can be examined and consciously negotiated by the writer, if s/he becomes aware of them.[20]

In order to teach student writers to be aware of and to participate in particular discourse communities—in particular, the discourse community of the writing classroom—Bartholomae suggests that writing teachers approach student texts by being what he calls "dismissive." He states,

> In the course that I teach, I begin by *not* granting the writer her 'own' presence in that paper, by denying the paper's status as a record to her own thoughts and feelings. I begin instead by asking her to read her paper as a text already written by the culture, representing a certain predictable version of the family, the daughter, and the writer. ("Response" 85, emphasis in original)

What Bartholomae calls being "dismissive," I identify as part of the process of "critique," and that larger process of critique works on many levels within the discourse communities operating in a writing class. For example, in the essay courses I teach, writers critique each other's work throughout the semester: we sit in a big circle and talk about each student's essay-draft to see where readers are in agreement, where we're confused, and where we disagree entirely about how each draft is working (in terms of content, organization, style, etc.). In essence, the class takes some of the ownership of the work accomplished in any particular student essay and of the insights, even, that are rendered in each.

Throughout the course of the semester, as part of the practice of critique, the students learn from me and from model texts the conventions of the form, what sorts of strategies generally work in the essay, what pitfalls to avoid, and how to comment on peers' essays. As part of that effort, they learn to identify hackneyed moves or insights in the drafts (what Bartholomae refers to, above, as claims that "represent a certain predictable version" of a topic), and we talk together about how to complicate them, how to push them so that the essay does more work.[21] As the semester progresses, I talk less and less, while they learn to catch the problems, point out strengths, and debate complexities on their own. In these ways, they learn the conventions and practices of engagement (both oral and written) within an essay class, within a writers' workshop, and within an essay. In turn, they learn to 'participate,' as Bartholomae calls it, with greater intensity, as the semester progresses, in the discourses driving the work of and circulating in our course.

Participation/critique does not, however, simply involve my training student essayists in the conventions and practices of the particular discourse communities at work in the essay course. For those who are invested in the concept of the socially constructed self and the written voice of that self on the page, it involves, in theory, students being trained to identify and comprehend their own construction, which is dictated by the conventions and practices of relevant discourse communities. So, in order to raise their awareness around that construction in this essay course, I'd have to do some work around how the conventions and practices involved in reading and writing essays both enable and limit their engagement with the genre, enable and limit what shows up in their own essays, as well as how the coursework both enables and limits the ways in which they function as individual identities in the classroom and on the page.

Participation/critique also involves my providing writers with the critical skills to refuse these conventions and practices—to break, perhaps, with a convention in an essay or to read an essay through the lens of a different tradition or theory, as I will do in this chapter. Thus, according to this conception of the writer-page relation, student essayists can and should be trained to write against the "norm" that may dictate the shape and content of their selves and their essays. Only then will they be able to find ways to critically participate in discourse communities in the ways in which Bartholomae refers. Only then will they be given the means to resist the forces that are working on them and that have made them complicit in the truths of a "society" (e.g., a classroom); only then will they be able to develop more autonomous voices on the page.

In his article "Writing with Teachers," Bartholomae figures this particular kind of participation in a classroom as a "contact zone," where the classroom functions as a space for critical inquiry, a space within which to discover strategies and to learn practices for critiquing the homogenizing and/or intrusive conventions and practices of discourse communities (66), while also learning to deploy them, as one wishes or chooses. By considering the essay as a space of critical inquiry, as a contact zone, the writer-page relationship is essentially remade—made in decidedly different ways from the processes described in Chapter 1. Here, the essay becomes a space where the same [social, political, and historical] conventions and practices that construct the flesh-and-blood writer are brought, by the writer, into contact within a complex of power structures on the page.

RE-PRESENTING THE SOCIAL SELF IN WRITING

The often cited example of a contact zone discussed by Mary Louise Pratt in "Arts of the Contact Zone," involves an Andean (Guaman Poma), who wrote a text that does not simply "imitate or reproduce" the "representational repertoire of the invaders," but "selects and adapts it along Andean lines to express [...]

Andean interests and aspirations" (36). This practice (of selecting and adapting) is an example of transculturation: "processes whereby members of subordinated or marginal groups select and invent from materials transmitted by a dominant or metropolitan culture" (36). The process of selecting and adapting "materials transmitted by a dominant [...] culture" is equal to the work of participation/critique described above: in it, students should select, by writing about, the materials of culture (e.g., the clichéd, popular understandings of complex issues as divorce or gun control) but turn them on their heads in order to resist them and to construct a more autonomous self. In trying to teach essays this way, however, I have found that the practice of "re-presenting," which seems central to any writing task in a contact zone, involves the operations of objectification and transcendence, and these operations make any writing task in a contact zone ultimately impotent in making change—e.g., in creating a more autonomous self.

Writers in/of contact zones *re-present* their real (as in living) selves on the page. To do so, they hone their awareness of the social categories and power structures that work on their real selves. Then, they carefully and responsibly select and adapt those social categories and power structures and reconstruct them on the page in the form of a textual world in which the writer's textual self lives. For example, in Pratt's use of Poma's text, she shows that he "construct[s] a new picture of the world, a picture of a Christian world with Andean rather than European peoples at the center of it" (34). Poma has selected the social categories of "Andean" and "European"; he has placed them in a world he has constructed in such a way that their power structure is inverted. In the process, he has also constructed a textual self that is the same but different when compared to his real self: it is a self that has resisted (by inverting) the real power structure in which the real Poma lives (which is, of course, a fiction), but that self is also, decidedly, "him."

To break Poma's process of critique down into observable steps, I suggest the following explanation: first, he identifies, from a subject-object position, what "The Andean" is and what "The European" is; then, he chooses what parts of each he'd like to put on the page; finally, he puts them into a relationship that is critical of the real-world relation between the two. Through this process, in a rather confusing twist, Poma gets to have it both ways—or four ways, to be more precise: he constructs on the page the subject (himself), which is, according to Pratt, equal to Poma-the-real-person but also equal to the more general category of the Andean; in his rendering of this individual/group identity within an inverted binary (the Andean and the Spaniard), he has made that identity both authentic in its relation to the real-world power structures, as well as critical of the same power structures by revising them in the text. All of this, he manages by pretending to work from outside of the actual power structures within which he lives, stepping outside of them in order to identify, assess, and reconstruct them on the page, like a god creating a world instead of like a citizen utterly inundated and made ("constructed") by the very structures he is critiquing.

Confusions aside and at the risk of sounding biting, it seems clear enough to me that rather than create an autonomous and critical self that is no longer complicit in the undesirable social forces working on him, as Bartholomae and others invested in critique may hope for, Poma has not done much more than imagine a simpler self living in a simpler world (simple, in part, because each culture has been reduced to a social category rendered within a binary). The failure of the text to accomplish the intended end of critique is due, in part, to the objectification at work in the process of re-presentation (of self, of cultures, etc.). To explain, I point to another excerpt from "Arts of the Contact Zone" in which Pratt asserts that "[i]n so far as anything is known about him at all, Guaman Poma exemplified the sociocultural complexities produced by conquest and empire" (34). In this statement, Pratt suggests that: 1. Poma, the flesh-and-blood man, is equal to the historical and political context within which he lived, and 2. the textual Poma is a kind of micropicture of the same "picture of the world" that he constructs in the text.

The problem with these assumptions and with the steps I described above is that they are, to use Nietzsche's famous accusation, "arrogant": in reducing what is necessarily complex and infinitely various to these easy social categories and, then, by asserting/assuming that the process of constructing this reductive re-presentation makes the writer's self stronger, more autonomous in the real (complex) world. To recognize this arrogance is, I think, to ask certain questions: How can a single individual "exemplify" a culture? How can any human being (or group of human beings, for that matter) adequately capture and re-present on the page an entire culture? How can any individual decide which forces will act on him/her—whether in "real life" or on a page? Such powers would suggest the existence and work of a kind of superhuman (and, I should note, not the kind that I think Nietzsche is after in the figure of Zarathustra): one who is incredibly aware and in-control of his/her own "social-ness" to the extent that s/he can make herself/himself true to or impervious to certain social forces, to the extent that s/he can, in fact, wield those social forces.

The point is that the assumptions that drive this concept of the socially constructed self and its re-presentation on the page hinge on a process in which the socially conscious and rhetorically savvy writer can transcend the social categories and power structures within which s/he lives, identify from that position those that s/he wants to re-present in writing, and then, revise the ways in which they function by re-presenting them in critical ways on the page. Because of these assumptions, this conception of the socially constructed self of the writer and his/her re-presentation on the page smacks of the same problems described in the first chapter of this project—problems that stem from a conception of self that perpetuates the myth of transcendence.

THE DETERMINISTIC INFLUENCES OF DISCOURSE COMMUNITIES AND THE POWER OF CHOICE

A few scholars (e.g., Patricia Bizzell) have reminded us that though an "aware" writer (like Poma) might be able to choose how s/he appropriates and re-presents the conventions and practices of particular discourse communities, we don't have a choice as to what discourses we are subjected to; at best, we can only choose among those that are available to us (see Bizzell's "What Is a Discourse Community"). For scholars like Pratt and Bartholomae, who are interested in the concept of the contact zone, and for essayists and essay teachers who, in turn, may be interested in the essay functioning like a contact zone, the key to writing critically is choice, itself: through it, the essayist can overcome the otherwise unstoppable influence of "society." For example, in the popular creative nonfiction textbook, *Shadow Boxing*, Molly Ivins's "Texas Women: True Grit and All the Best" explores what are essentially the various discourse communities of Texan women, though she doesn't call them "discourse communities"; rather, she presents several "strains" of Texan culture that determine Texas Womanhood. Via these "strains," Texas women have a few possibilities (choices) within which their womanhood can be constructed.

Ivins states, "As has been noted elsewhere, there are several strains of Texan culture: They are all rotten for women." They include (among others) the Southern belle of Confederate heritage, who is the flirtatious "woman-on-a-pedestal"; the "pervasive good-ol'-boyism of *Redneckus texensis*," which maintains the virgin/whore dichotomy; and "the legacy of the frontier," where the "little ladies" are protected by "the big, strong man" (53-54). Texan culture is divided into perceivable and broadly applicable categories within which women's roles are determined by the conventions and practices of each. Those conventions and practices are suggested in the categories themselves (e.g., the "woman-on-a-pedestal" is idealized by others), so I won't focus on these here. Instead, what seems most important to this discussion is that Ivins suggests in her essay that a woman's personality is in some way, if not in all ways, determined by the discourse community to which she chooses to belong: e.g., she can either be a "woman-on-a-pedestal" or a "little lady."

Given the limiting and insidious nature of the conventions and practices of these particular discourse communities, it would not be too difficult to argue that any female subject in any one of them would be entirely regulated/controlled by

Chapter Two

those conventions and practices. In an interesting move toward the end of the essay, however, Ivins states, "Texas women are just as divided by race, class, age, and educational level as are other varieties of human beings," (55) which seems to be an admission of what could be, what are, far more complex subjectivities living in these discourse communities. Nevertheless, Ivins continues a sentence later: "There's a pat description of 'what every Texas woman wants' that varies a bit from city to city, but the formula that Dallas females have been labeled goes something like this [...]" (55). Oddly, despite Ivins's admission that women are "just as divided" by other social categories, she swiftly moves into further categorization in the "pat description" of Texas women's wants and offers no critique of that description. I suspect that this is because a critique of such a generalization would disable the operation of objectification: it would unravel her claim that this particular group of women is determined by the conventions (in this case, the desires) of its respective discourse community. To put this another way, there can be no critique of a discourse community, no selecting and adapting, no choice among and within them, if there are no consistent and identifiable qualities to delineate one community from another.

As many scholars have already argued, though, discourse communities consist of more than one, agreed-upon set of rules and practices.[22] This is even demonstrated in Ivins's articulation of several competing strains of Texan culture that are all operating within the larger discourse community of Texan women. Such contradictions/conflicts are so normal that in Ivins's essay, for example, it is not difficult for the reader to accept the following tensions: that though they are the victims of pervasive sexism, Texan women are also "tough in some very fundamental ways" (56); and that despite her awareness of the sexism behind notions of Texas Womanhood, Ivins at one point adhered to it. However, in order to critique a discourse community, one must be able to identify it according to at least a few generalizable conventions, and in that generalization, the writer in/of a contact zone erases complexity, objectifies a community, and moves into a [false] transcendent position. Ivins, in fact, confesses that she can opt out of these discourse communities because she is "more of an observer" (52). Consequently, she is both able to play the critic and able to construct a subject-on-the-page that is not determined by any of the strains of Texan culture that she has re-presented.

According to composition and essay scholars who are invested in this socially constructed concept of the self, in order to "participate" critically in discourse communities, writers must become observers, thus transcending the discourse community in question by enacting a subject-to-object relation to it. More specifically, writers in/of contact zones find criteria by which they can categorize a discourse community; only then can they betray those criteria, choose to write against those criteria, e.g., by creating a self-on-the-page that rejects conventions and practices of the Texan "little lady" or of the oppressed Andean. Again, the supposed benefit of the objectifying and transcending move is that if they learn the practice well, writers can step far enough away from the culture that is imposed on them to construct a self that has more agency with regards to that culture.

WHERE THE CONTACT ZONE FAILS US

In an example meant to stand as a recommendation to all teachers of writing, Bartholomae states that he encourages one of his writers "to revise in such a way that the order of the essay is broken—to write against the grain of the discourse that has determined her account of her family" ("Response" 85). He doesn't say what the student's representative narrative is, but if one follows his cue that this student has written a paper about her parents' divorce, then chances are good that she's done the work through one of the more normative binaries, perhaps like the following: divorce is good because it gives couples the choice to find a better/different life, or it's bad because it gives couples the choice to "give up" on their life together.

Bartholomae is also not specific about what a paper that "works against the grain of the discourse that has determined her account" would look like; however, to use the example above, the student might look closely at the values and assumptions at work in both sides of the binary: that divorce is necessarily good or bad and how her position as daughter, as young female, as member of the middle class, etc., influences her evaluation of divorce as good or bad. The irony is that in order to be capable of writing against one deterministic discourse, the student writer must write within the conventions and practices of another discourse. For example, the student whose paper is described above would have to learn how to talk about "assumptions," how to critically engage "evaluative terms," how to problematize binaries, and so on.

In a more explicit example of this movement between the conventions of a couple of discourse communities (i.e., using the conventions of one in order to critique another), I point to Linda Brodkey's essay "Writing on the Bias." In it, she writes about her inundation in the conventions of academic speak, or what she calls "objective" language. She finds that in actuality, the objective, which she explains as a middle class convention, is a lie, ultimately an impossibility.[23] In contrast, Brodkey states, "[Writing on the bias] recognizes the third dimension of seemingly two-dimensional material" (547). That "third dimension" is the subjective orientation to a topic, experience, idea, argument, etc. For Brodkey, her family's economic class and her subsequent orientation to the middle class

Chapter Two

(her membership in both would constitute a "contact zone") are part of her subjective approach and, ultimately, decide for her how she can and must write. The third dimension of her writing, comes from her orientations to these two economic classes—orientations she feels she can choose between, since she now recognizes that the objective (a "middle-class construct"), for example, often stands in for "reality," when it actually works to squash or "silence" the experience of "other quarters" (547). Thus, in her essay, Brodkey says "yes," by giving voice to her own bias and, in turn, says "no" by refusing the oppressive conventions of objective language.

In this example, again, the assumption seems to be that a writer can not only recognize what social influences are at work on his/her self and on a group of people, but s/he can also say "yes" or "no" to them in a text. Saying "yes" or "no" suggests that the operations of objectification and transcendence are at work again, for the writer is assumed to be able to observe the social influences at work on him/her from a subject-to-object relation and to decide which social forces to implicate in the self-on-the-page. The problem is that by saying "no" to one set of conventions, we can only do so by deploying another set of conventions; critique doesn't happen in a vacuum after all. It must always happen within particular power relations, which are already in existence and operating within and among discourses long before any individual writer or essayist picks up a pen or faces a cursor. In Brodkey's case, she writes in the conventions and practices of one discourse ("the subjective" or what rhetoric and composition scholars and teachers might recognize as "the personal") when she chooses not to write in the objective. Thus, there is no moment of transcendence over/beyond social forces, when the writer says "yes" or "no." To assume that we can transcend is deeply problematic; in fact, the element of choice, itself, is also deeply problematic.

These problems are brought home in decidedly powerful ways in Richard Miller's article, "Fault Lines in the Contact Zone." Miller describes a situation where a student realizes that in order to read the work of Anzaldúa, whom the student initially brands a "femo-nazi" (among other pejorative markers), he would have to "set aside [his] personal values, outlook and social position in order to escape the bars of being offended and discouraged" (406). Though Miller seems to see this admission as progress, I would argue that it is based on the false assumption that one is capable of "setting aside" (of transcending) personal values, social position, etc. Perhaps more importantly, Miller's use of the example as a positive point of change suggests that this "setting aside" *should* be done—e.g., that Anzaldua's work should no longer be read within the dynamics of racism and sexism, dynamics that are essential to the work of the text. To ignore them, to displace them, is to deny the work its own fabric, its own constitution, as well as the writer's own fabric and constitution. Worse, the effort to ignore, displace, and "transcend" accomplishes absolutely nothing in changing the power relations at work in the reader-text encounter. For example, in this case, the student only manages to compartmentalize his prejudice for the sake of an exercise—a process that is, frankly, no more than a grand pretend.

In the field of Rhetoric and Composition's turn to "the social," as Patricia Bizzell calls it, this belief in a scholar's (and potentially, a student's) ability to "set aside" his/her own subjectivity is a common one. In fact, scholars and students are often required to deploy this skill—transcending social context—a skill that stems from an institutionalized belief that Stanley Fish calls "theory hope." As Bizzell explains the concept, "The tendency […] is to hope that by becoming aware of the personal, social, and historical circumstances that constitute our beliefs, we can achieve a critical distance on them and change our beliefs if we choose" ("Foundationalism" 205). In other words, some of us—and some of our students—believe that by becoming aware of the construction of our subject positions within/according to discourses on gender, for example, we can decide to no longer be gendered—except, perhaps, according to our own preferences.

Perhaps it's obvious why such a belief would be problematic, but to quote Bizzell again, the reason is because "no theory can achieve transcendence of, and explanatory power over, the discourse in which it is framed" ("Foundationalism" 215). No individual can achieve that transcendence either. Even when we examine how individuals function within discourses concerned with gender, sexuality, race, etc., that examination occurs (is deployed) within and according to discourses always, already at work. I, for example, don't get to just invent a whole new discourse from and within which to talk about the essay. Rather, I must work within discourses that already exist, that are operating in every sentence, indeed in the language, of this project. In other words, there is no way "out"—however much we'd like to believe there is.

WHERE TO NOW

That said, just because the concept of the socially constructed self is a pawn in an impossible game, where players believe themselves capable of objectifying and transcending culture and their selves in order to (re)construct and re-present them on a page, that doesn't mean we should throw out all practices that are part of the processes of self-examination and social-awareness. Instead, the question intensifies: how can we, teachers of the essay, empower student essayists without asking them to practice the impossible, transcendent move that is enabled by a belief in an essential self or a socially constructed self?

I don't think the answer to this problem lies in identifying social categories, reversing power structures, or trying/hoping to write from outside of our own social construction. In fact, I would steer clear of the question that Robertson and Martin pose in "Culture as Catalyst and Constraint": "[…W]ho is in charge of what or whom, through what means, and toward what ends?" (507). Their question hinges on the belief that if people can figure out who is constraining whom, then out of mutual respect and continued confrontation, people can make a "genuine change" (509). The problem with this belief is it misleads writers into thinking they can rise "above" their social-ness, above the page, above the discourses at work at any given moment, even above their own selves, manifested in flesh or in black squiggles on white pages. Somehow, it invites or encourages the assumption that if we are constructed, then we are constructed like a house—and that the solution to any power structure problem is really just a matter of moving things around—which is, frankly, overly simplistic. We miss the mark (and likely get ourselves into trouble) if we assume that we can just accept or reject social influences ("I will not be gendered today!") or that the game will fundamentally change with another captain calling the shots or, worse, that we can change the game from the sidelines.

The bottom line is that in the conceptualization of subjectivity I've traced out in this chapter, the writer, the essayist, is privileged as the creator, conveyor, tyrant of the text and of the self that may show up on a page. Consequently, I would argue that those of us who may have bought into this conceptualization of the self are only inviting the same sort of tyranny, the sort of self-serving engagement that I saw in the student essay I described at the beginning of this chapter. Couldn't he argue that he has rejected the prudish codes of conduct and attitudes of one discourse community in order to affirm a different set of codes and attitudes? If so, then not enough has changed in the shift from one conception of the writer-page relation to the other. As such, I propose that we ask, instead, what would happen if we worked from the assumption that the subject is not the originator, not the creator, not the actor—at least not in the "arrogant" ways in which we like to pretend that s/he is. How might a subject *be constituted* in a text, i.e., how is a subject constituted in discourses (e.g., of the essay), in the practices at work in those discourses? And, how might the writer participate in that constituting? In other words, how can we (re)conceptualize subjectivity in the essay in terms that are not reducible to the "old shoe" binary of the essential self v. the socially constructed self?

NOTES

15. I think it worth noting that Bartholomae's production (with Anthony Petrosky) of *Ways of Reading* suggests that he, in fact, does think his students capable of being "elegant [and] smart." The textbook incorporates readings that many first-year

writing teachers would probably see as too sophisticated, too dense, for first-year writers. Yet, here are Bartholomae and Petrosky on the matter: "[...T]his is why a course in reading is also a course in writing. Our students need to learn that there is something they can do once they have first read through a complicated text; successful reading is not just a matter of 'getting' an essay the first time. In a very real sense, you can't begin to feel the power a reader has until you realize the problems, until you realize that no one 'gets' Geertz or Rich or Griffin or Wideman all at once. You work on what you read, and then what you have at the end is something that is yours, something you made" (vii). Clearly, Bartholomae thinks students capable of elegant and smart work, work that at least approximates the scholar's.

16. See, for example, recent discussions on the WPA listserv about the value of personal writing (a search for "personal writing" in the listserv archives will bring up those discussions).

17. Regarding the value of readers' responses, Elbow does not throw the baby out with the bathwater. There is value for the reader in the writer's process, but that role is significantly different from the reader-as-critic that I will describe in this chapter. In *Writing Without Teachers*, Elbow discusses at length the value of receiving peer feedback, i.e., "movies of the mind" from readers, so that the writer, then, can have a clearer understanding of how her work is managing her intentions—if readers are getting from her writing what she wants them to get from it or not. She is then supposed to use this feedback to make adjustments to her work so that it aligns better with her intentions. There is also Elbow's work on the believing/doubting game in which writers challenge and take seriously their own claims—i.e., they play critics to their own works. Both seem to be strategies for encouraging the writer to take full ownership of the text, even of its critique. The major difference in Bartholomae's and Elbow's notions of critique seems obvious enough: the former sees it as being most productive if it is rendered by one who understands the topics, values, and beliefs at stake, as well as the discourse within which they are circulating, better than the writer; the former sees critique as being most productive if it is owned (if not rendered from, then accepted or rejected) by the writer.

18. Admittedly, Bartholomae is focused here on what should go on in a first-year composition classroom: what kind of writing should be privileged, what kind of relationship we should be teaching our students to have to their texts, what kind of work they should be doing as writers, etc. Perhaps, as a consequence, it could be argued that the kinds of writers or written selves that are taken up in the debate between Bartholomae and Elbow have little to do with the self of the essayist/essay. I understand this argument, but I disagree. Granted, the goal of Elbow's classroom (to teach students to express themselves) is different from Bartholomae's (to teach students to critique culture). On the other hand, these goals are driven by the same impetus—an interest in "student rights" (see Jeanette Harris), or more specifically, an interest in students' empowerment, which hinges on concepts of agency. I would

argue that essayists have the very same interest.

I, as an essayist, admittedly come at my own empowerment, my own agency, through different means in an essay, than I do as a scholar in my scholarship. I'm addressing a different audience and am expected to work within different genre conventions. However, the basic assumptions about the writer-page relation that are at work in conversations about one genre can speak to those that are at work in conversations about other kinds of writing. For example, is it not interesting that in Technical Writing, the student is expected to keep his/her voice "out" of the writing? Is it not interesting, too, that in a composition course, voice teachers teach students to "find their voices"? The question then becomes: what is the writer-page relationship in each?

To put this in more explicit and applicable terms, it is easy to read the Elbow-Bartholomae debate as one of missed lines, i.e., as a debate over totally separate issues: voice and critique. However, I'd argue that the two interests are not mutually exclusive in a personal essay, for how critique is conducted has much to do with how a subject is believed to be reflected/constructed on a page and vice versa. This symbiotic relationship—between subjectivity and critique—will become clearer throughout the course of this chapter, but for the time being, it should suffice to say that what composition teachers have to say about voice and writing speaks in interesting ways to what essayists have to say about voice and the essay and vice versa. This conversation is worth pursuing in order to discover what the implications of it are, and that pursuit is exactly the impetus behind this chapter.

19. Two particularly interesting works of scholarship that take up the issue of a socially constructed self in personal writing are as follows: Stuart Ching's "Memory as Travel," which engages the problematic relationship in creative nonfiction of memory and narrative in a socially constructed identity; and Elisabeth Leonard's "Assignment #9," which is an example and exploration of "experimental" writing that specifically engages the concept of a socially constructed self.

20. I hesitate to use the term "discourse communities" because as Joseph Harris says of the latter term "community," "there is something maddening and vague about the term" ("Community" 6). Given the concession in the field about how "we write not as isolated individuals but as members of communities whose beliefs, concerns, and practices both instigate and constrain" (Harris *Teaching* 98), though, I have chosen to stick to the term "discourse community." However, I will use this term in a pointed way: in order to set up and analyze how the concept of "contact zones" works, a concept that at least professes to disrupt the tyrannizing concept and influence of discourse communities.

I understand and deploy the term "discourse communities" according to the work of Bartholomae and of Patricia Bizzell. Bizzell, in her article "Cognition, Convention, and Certainty," explains the concept as such: "Groups of society members can become accustomed to modifying each other's reasoning and language use in certain ways. Eventually, these familiar ways achieve the status of conventions that bind the group in a discourse community, at work together on some project of interaction with the material world" (214). One such project of interaction with the material world is, of course, the writing classroom.

21. What they learn, too, and what they comment on most to me with each new round of drafts is that a lot of the students' essays "sound the same." That is, my students begin to see the very issues that Bartholomae complains of in "Writing With Teachers," but for them, the stakes are not so much about participating differently in order to practice critique effectively; rather, for them, the stakes are about doing "something different." They are pointedly, even passionately, interested in creating works that stand out, that are remarkable.

22. For example, Patricia Bizzell argues, "Healthy discourse communities, like healthy human beings, are also masses of contradictions" ("What" 235). Or to quote Pratt, "People and groups are constituted not by single unified belief systems, but by competing self-contradicting ones" ("Interpretive" 228). These competing beliefs do not change a discourse community's ability to be recognized as a unit, though. As Harris states, "One does not need consensus to have community" (*Teaching* 106).

23. Incidentally, this is often the rally-cry for many creative nonfiction advocates (for example, see Lynn Z. Bloom's "Living to Tell the Tale").

CHAPTER 3: CULTIVATING A SELF IN THE ESSAY

> We take the opinions and the knowledge of others into our keeping, and that is all. We must make them our own. We are just like a man who, needing fire, should go and find some at his neighbor's house, and, having found a fine big fire there, should stop there and warm himself, forgetting to carry any back home. What good does it do to us to have our belly full of meat if it is not digested, if it is not transformed into us, if it does not make us bigger and stronger?
>
> - Michel de Montaigne, "Of Pedantry"

As I mentioned at the beginning of Chapter 2, not long ago, I had a student who jeered at the rape and murder of women in the essays he submitted to me and to the class. When I first met with the student to talk about the content in his essays, he was hostile: "But this is who I really am!" he exclaimed. "I have a twisted sense of humor!" In taking this case to several of my rhetoric and composition colleagues, the most consistent bit of advice I got from them was to steer the student away from thinking about his self-on-the-page as a constitutive act of voice (an expression or a textual re-presentation of the "real" writer) and, instead, as a construction of ethos. With this shift in perspective, the assumption was that he would be able to see the self-on-the-page as his audience might see it. Then, we could talk about the ineffectiveness of that ethos and about how to revise so that the essay's ethos would be more effective. Of course, what was implied in their advice, too, was that the student would then see the error of his ways, for inevitably, he would find that the more effective ethos would be one that aligned with the values, morals, and codes of conduct deemed acceptable by an audience of me and of upper-level English majors.

The problem with this implication is, I hope, obvious: that the student would be required to conform to institutionally accepted values, if he wanted to produce an effective essay. This would not necessarily be a problem if those values only involved his use of the conventions of a "good" essay—e.g., those mentioned in Chapter 1 (freedom, walking, and voice). Instead, in this particular case, what counted as a good/effective essay involved the rendering of a particular kind of voice or textual self—one that embodied the values and ethical practices that would be deemed appropriate, that would be accepted by a group of his peers and by me. Consequently, by asking the student to examine the ethos in his writing in order to deploy it more effectively, I would not have been asking him simply to reflect further (on) the voice-on-the-page or his textual self; I would have been teaching him to align his voice/textual self with particular socio-political values so that the ethos would be perceived to be reliable.[24] As such, I would have become a part of a system where the disciplining practices of our field take a turn toward the silencing practices of intellectual tyranny—just the sort of practices with which any voice scholar and/or teacher would take serious issue.

No doubt, one could argue (as I often do, myself) that it's more important to teach students to be attentive, respectful, socially-responsible, and critical thinkers than it is to give them the space to "be their own persons," which in my student's case, would translate to being a person who participates in and perpetuates some of the most horrible 'isms' that exist today. Yet, doesn't that privileging fly in the face of the real work of the personal essay as the last "free" space for self-expression? Perhaps even more importantly, by teaching said values, how am I much better than the kind of person whose ideology I'm trying to disempower?

Certainly, I know—and can argue—the difference between the self-righteousness that I am invoking and the self-righteousness articulated in the rape-celebrating essay written by my student. I can argue that in asking my student to revise the ethos of his essay and that in explaining why he needs to revise that ethos, I would be inserting myself into discourses that perpetuate dangerous hierarchies and abuse; I would be trying to create a disruption, trying to break a chain forged over centuries of problematic thinking, talking, and acting along perilous conceptions of gender roles. But after making such attempts over a decade of teaching, I know for certain that if students read such an attempt as me trying to silence them, then my attempts at "disruption" only persuade them to shut down the exchange (and, ironically, often in the name of "self-expression").

In part, the problem seems to stem from our modern-day conceptions of self. To be more specific, as Crowley and Hawhee explain to rhetoric and writing students in their textbook *Ancient Rhetorics for Contemporary Students*, "Americans tend to link a person's opinions to her identity. We assume that someone's opinions result from her personal experience, and hence that those opinions are somehow 'hers'—that she alone 'owns' them" (5). Thus, folks tend to get very upset when their opinions are challenged because the assumption is that their opinions are not all that is at stake in a discussion; their identities, their selfhoods, are.

The presence of this assumption about opinion-as-identity in personal essay courses, in writing pedagogies, and even in writing and essay scholarship is, arguably, the residual effect of an institutional purchase of (with all the associated advertising for) romanticism and its hero, the romantic subject. Borrowing the wording of John Muckelbauer in his work on imitation (and the humanities' resistance to it), we are seeing the effects of "the institutional emergence of romantic subjectivity, an ethos that emphasizes *creativity, originality,* and *genius*" (52, emphasis added). One of those effects can be seen in the fact that conceptions of the essayist, especially, are bound up in the belief in "opinion-as-identity."

To explain with regards to agency, as it is forwarded in Chapters 1 and 2, if we buy the concept of the essential or socially constructed self, then we tend to see our subjectivities as entirely dependent on our ability to *have* and to interpret our experiences, as if *how* we experience and *what* we experience happen in a subject-object relation (i.e., me vs. the experience). When we enter into a relation with the object-that-is-experience, we interpret it and become, in that act, agents that can control it. In this relation, "life" becomes a series of events to be interpreted. We possess those interpretations by imposing on them a narrative (enter "creativity") that is the product of our unique perspective (enter "originality"), which is unique because of the unique constellation of experiences that have been interpreted by our individual selves (enter "genius").[25]

The upshot of this tangle is that we get to see ourselves as agents in this world—not simply as actors but as unique entities that necessarily interpret and possess experience differently. What we also get is the belief that my perspective is who I am and that any challenge to that perspective—which, ironically, can be represented by groups to which I belong, e.g., institutions, families, etc.—is a threat to my very existence. One can easily see this belief in opinion-as-identity at work in my student's argument for his voice, his true/honest self, on the page. One can easily see it in the failed attempts on my part to interject in a discourse in which that voice is implicated.

If we give in to the "implacable I" of the essayist, as Joan Didion calls it, or the "it's all about me ethic," as I called it in Chapter 2, and if we, consequently, dismiss any responsibility to the people who may be belittled or silenced by that implacability, then just how valuable can the essay really be? What is it likely to contribute to any discourse it participates in? Is it likely to be rigorous, skeptical, profound? I'd argue "no" because, contrary to popular belief, the essay would not be freed by the essentialized or socially-constructed self that is expressed or re-presented in an essay; rather, the essay would be limited by that self—and in dangerous ways.

For the purposes of this chapter, then, I would like "to make visible a bygone way of approaching the self and others which might suggest possibilities for the present" (Rabinow xxvii)—in particular, possibilities for how one might conceive of subjectivity in the essay. To do this work, I turn to the work of Michel Foucault. The practices that will be examined in this chapter are described best in Foucault's piece, titled "Self Writing." In it, he introduces self writing as a series of practices in which the writer participates in order to constitute and "cultivate" his/her self. Through this exploration of Foucault's work on subjectivity, I hope to describe a compelling and progressive study of subjectivity in essaying, one that enables productive debate and, even, self-transformation, one that does not send writers right back into the traps created by the theories of the writer-page relationship that I articulated in the first two chapters of this project.

Foucault's work, however, only provides the system of thought—the skeleton, so to speak, around which one can shape the conception/articulation of an actual subject-in-writing. In order to provide a few subjects-in-writing in which to examine relevant writing practices and in order to flesh-out this particular version of subjectivity, I have chosen to take up the essays of Montaigne. I've chosen his works for at least a few important reasons: the most important reason being that Montaigne is considered the "father" of the genre; the second reason being that his essays are often quoted to support each of the conceptions of the relationship between the writer and the self-on-the-page that I described in Chapters 1 and 2. As I will demonstrate, however, reading his essays as evidence of either conception of that relationship is a misreading, and as such, we have missed a very real, very productive possibility for conceiving of that relationship in the essay.

SELF WRITING

In "Self Writing," Foucault looks at "the role of writing in philosophical cultivation of the self just before Christianity: its close link with companionship, its application to the impulses of thought, its role as a truth test" (208). Specifically, he studies the practices of self writing in the works of Seneca, Plutarch, and Marcus Aurelius. What he finds is that the "close link with companionship," as well as self writing's "application to the impulses of thought" and "its role as a truth test," are all elements found in the works of these writers. These three elements should sound familiar to essayists and essay scholars, for essay writing involves conversing with the writer and with a reader (companionship), expressing or constructing "the mind on the page" (the application of writing to the impulses of thought), and experimenting with and/or exploring ideas (truth tests). The difference, though, between Foucault's articulation of these elements and more common articulations is that the former involves the privileging of practices—of conversing, of applying, of testing—not the sovereignty of the writer, as the creator of companionship, as the creator of the application of writing to thought, as the creator of the truth test.

To explain, much of Foucault's work focuses on several modes of objectivation, modes through which the subject "subjects" his/her self. "Subjecting," however, does not simply imply "making into an object," as the term "objectification" might suggest. Rather, a different process happens in that subjecting, so that the subject-on-the-page is constituted, not reflected or constructed. The distinction I want to make here between "constituted" and "constructed" is one of agency: i.e., saying a subject is "constructed" puts more emphasis on the writer (or the culture) that is doing the constructing, while "constituted" emphasizes the processes of subjection, the practices within which a subject is subjected.[26]

For example, the practices of self writing, at least pre-Christian self writing, are driven not by the creative genius or essence of the expressive writer but by the cultivation of "the art of living."[27] Foucault argues that according to the Pythagoreans, the Socratics, and the Cynics, "the art of living" can only be acquired with exercise, via "a training of the self by oneself" ("Self Writing" 208). This training is a way of caring for the self. Foucault states, "In Greek and Roman texts, the injunction of having to know yourself was always associated with the other principle of having to take care of yourself, and it was that need to care for oneself that brought the Delphic maxim [Know thyself] into operation" ("Technologies" 20). In other words, self writing is not simply the process of figuring out what I already know, who I already am. Rather, care of the self, which involves multiple practices that shape the self, makes possible knowledge of one's self. In the ancient world, such practices often included the use of *hupomnēmata*, which, according to Foucault, were written for the purpose of meditation; as I will show, this, too, is precisely what Montaigne's essays were written for.

THE HUPOMNĒMATA

Examples of *hupomnēmata* include "account books, public registers, or individual notebooks serving as memory aids." These memory aids were used, though, not simply for the purpose of aiding memory but for the primary purpose of being "guides for conduct" ("Self Writing" 209). In "Self Writing" Foucault states, "They constituted a material record of things read, heard, or thought, thus offering them up as a kind of accumulated treasure for subsequent reading and meditation" (209). He explains further that they were "a material and a framework" for the exercises of "reading, rereading, meditating, [and] conversing with oneself and with others" (210). In other words, these texts were not written out, (re)read, and referenced simply for the sake of recollection but, to quote Plutarch, to "[elevate] the voice and [silence] the passions like a master who with one word hushes the growling of dogs" (qtd. in "Self Writing" 210). So, for example, in high school, I kept a quote journal, which was comprised of lines from texts I found to be particularly compelling. I returned to them when

I needed them—usually for ideas for paper topics, but also for good advice when confronting complicated situations in my personal relationships, schooling, etc. This is [a simplification of] what I think Plutarch meant by "hush[ing] the growling of dogs"—the dogs, in this case, being conflicts and deadlines, for example.

The primary purpose, however, of the *hupomnēmata* is "to make one's recollection of the fragmentary *logos* transmitted through teaching, listening, or reading, a means of establishing a relationship of oneself with oneself, a relationship as adequate and accomplished as possible" ("Self Writing" 211). As to how that collection becomes a means to establishing a relationship of oneself with oneself, the process is complicated. To start by putting this relationship into more general terms (and work down to the specifics), the truths constituted in these texts are—through the practice of meditation—"planted in" the soul: that is, "the soul must make them *not merely its own but itself*" ("Self Writing" 210, emphasis added). To understand this process and to practice it, one must shift away from thinking about subjectivity in terms of the socially constructed self or the natural/essential self, and toward a different version.

In these more common conceptions of self, the assumption that the soul makes these truths its own would have been true. Students would accept and own the truths they encounter in readings, or they would reject them. In turn, when writing about those truths, the writer would become the owner of those beliefs by interpreting and rendering them through his/her own unique perspective. However, in stating that the soul does not merely make particular truths its own but "makes them itself," the distinction is as follows: the soul does not create, possess, and/or wield truths; rather, the soul is *constituted in* the practices of reading, rereading, and writing about those truths.[28]

As shown in Chapter 1, essay writing is often used in contemporary writing classrooms as a tool for expressing the innermost self, as a tool for expressing what is hidden/secret, what is oppressed/silenced in the self—the "stuff" of the soul that we own but have not owned up to, so to speak. Despite this common conception of the essay, though, in Montaigne's work, expression does not actually seem to be the purpose. Rather, Montaigne's essays work much like the *hupomnēmata*, which were written "for a purpose that is nothing less than the shaping of the self" ("Self Writing" 211). Montaigne admits to this project in "Of Giving the Lie." He states,

> And if no one reads me, have I wasted my time […]? In modeling this figure [this book] upon myself, I have had to fashion and compose myself so often to bring myself out, that the model itself has to some extent grown firm and taken

> shape. Painting myself for others, I have painted my inward self with colors clearer than my original ones. I have no more made my book than my book has made me—a book consubstantial with its author [...]. (504)

In effect, he is saying that in writing his book, he's not expressed a self; instead, in writing his book, the writing has cultivated his self.[29]

THE PRACTICES OF READING AND WRITING: "RETURNING TO THE HIVE"

Montaigne further describes at least a part of this process as such: "I have not studied one bit to make a book; but I have studied a bit *because* I had made it, if it is studying a bit to skim over and pinch, by his head or his feet, now one author, now another..." ("Of Giving" 505, emphasis added). Accordingly, it is not that he simply studied other works and then wrote about them; rather, as I will show, in the making of the book, Montaigne meditated on other authors' works, and they became a part of the constitution of his book/self. For example, in "Of Books" he talks about "transplanting" original ideas (e.g., from the works of Seneca) into his own "soil" and "confound[ing]" them with his own (296).

In this context, I can imagine that the *hupomnēmata* can be used like personal diaries or writers' notebooks, much like Didion describes in "On Keeping a Notebook," where writers collect material for reflection and/or for future writings.[30] However, it's worth noting that there's a difference between collections like Didion's notebooks and my students' diaries. The latter, at least according to my students, are often simply collections of confessions, which have very little use-value beyond the act of confession (and in fact, are oftentimes impossible, even, to understand after any considerable lapse of time because of their opaquely self/situation-referential prose). The writer rarely returns to them. The *hupomnēmata*, on the other hand, are supposed to be guidebooks. As such, the students' confessions would have to be used for meditative purposes—as material to later reflect on (in reading and in writing), to test the truth of by recontextualizing them in other experiences/scenarios, and if necessary, to revise.

The *hupomnēmata* are not, however, just another practice in pop-psychology. They are not simply collections of affirmations I repeat to myself in order to feel okay about myself or my life. Rather, in the act of meditating on those texts, a disciplining, a cultivating, of self occurs, for in that act, a relationship of oneself with oneself is established, a relationship that should be "as adequate and accomplished as possible"—i.e., one that makes possible a relation between the two (subjected) subjects so that they work agonistically toward an end that belongs to "an ethics of control" (*Care* 65). This ethic in practice, in process, is a bit like Heracles wrestling the Nemean lion, which (if I may make a somewhat obscure reference) is described in *The Mythic Tarot* as a symbolic struggle between Heracles and his ego. It is an encounter of oneself to oneself, the latter of which is in relation to the former but not as its reflection, not even as its equal. Rather, the two are constituted in the encounter and struggle agonistically toward an end that is the conversion of the self. Thus, the end that belongs to an ethic of control is not an end where Heracles slays the lion or vice versa. Instead, he masters it. It is submitted, as is he, in the encounter that involves a series of practices—perhaps of tactical maneuvers of fatal bites and pinched veins. In fact, in Greene and Sharman-Burke's reading of the story in *The Mythic Tarot*, neither player can be negated or rejected; to convert/transform, neither can be killed.

To come at this relationship another way, one of the ways that one can cultivate that relationship so that it is "as adequate and accomplished as possible" is to practice "turning back," fixing the past in such a way that it can be studied. In this practice, the writer can, in turn, prepare for the future. To explain further this emphasis on composing a self capable of adapting to future events, I point to Foucault's analysis of dreams in the first chapter of *The Care of the Self*. There, he quotes from Achilles Tatius's *The Adventures of Leucippe and Clitophon* to show how the analysis of dreams was a life practice, practiced for the purpose not of controlling or outwitting one's destiny but of preparing for it. Tatius states, "[...F]or when disasters come all together and unexpectedly, they strike the spirit with so severe and sudden a blow that they overwhelm it; while if they are anticipated, the mind, by dwelling on them beforehand, is able little by little to turn the edge of sorrow" (5). This practice of studying dreams relates to the practice of self writing, for in both, the self is constituted within practices that are used for the purpose of disciplining the self—in this case, to discipline the self in order to abate sorrow or to avoid the debilitating effects of suffering.

In another example, in "Of Presumption" Montaigne states, "Not being able to rule events [or 'Fortune'], I rule myself, and adapt myself to them if they do not adapt themselves to me" (488). In other words, he cannot control the future, so instead, he cultivates a self that can adapt to the events that may happen in the future. In describing how one can work toward this self, in "Of Experience," Montaigne states, "He who remembers the evils he has undergone, and those that have threatened him, and the slight causes that have changed him from one state to another, prepares himself in that way for future changes and for recognizing his condition" (822). In that remembering, in meditating on the past, and in preparing for the future, he practices control, and because of it, he also will be able to practice control in whatever future struggles he encounters.

THE PRACTICES OF THE DISPARATE (THE TRUTH TEST)

To the question, again, then: How does one "write" the self, particularly a more vigilant or less susceptible self? In part, one does so by collecting material, reading it repeatedly, reflecting on it, and writing about it. However, that is not enough. In order for the writing to work—in order for it to actually create a more disciplined or at least a different self—the truths (the maxims) of the writings being meditated on and the truths generated in that meditation must be tested.

Again, self writing is not repeating affirmations ("I am a good scholar. I am a good scholar"). In order for it to work, in order for that relationship between writer and page to transform the self of the writer, truths (e.g., quotes from my quote-journal or entries from a student's diary) must be put to the test. Consequently, they are not "adopted" as the writer's own, but in the process of testing them, the writer is disciplined in them. To put this is Foucault's terms, "the writing of the *hupomnēmata* is also (and must remain) a regular and deliberate practice of the disparate" ("Self Writing 212). The "practice of the disparate" is a way "of combining the traditional authority of the already-said with the singularity of the truth that is affirmed therein and the particularity of the circumstances that determine its use" ("Self Writing" 212). In other words, writing becomes a practice of meditation in which the writer considers the selected passage as a maxim that may be true, suitable, and useful to a particular situation—or not. The purpose in practicing the disparate is mastery of the self—not via a conclusive and utterly naked revelation of self, as is so often argued about Montaigne's work, but "through the acquisition and assimilation of truth."

For example, in "Of Experience," Montaigne finds that in all of the interpretations that might occur in the "art" of language, there is not one universally "true" interpretation. However, this does not discourage him from the practice of the disparate, for while belying the possibility of clear, irrefutable meaning in the language-use of, say, lawyers and doctors, Montaigne quotes Seneca (which is an example of the already-said, of a maxim): "What is broken up into dust becomes confused" (816). He explores this maxim at length in the next paragraph, applying it to the language-use of lawyers in contract sand wills. In the end, he explains that by picking apart the language of such contracts and wills, by debating the meaning, "[lawyers] make the world fructify and teem with uncertainty and quarrels, as the earth is made more fertile the more it is crumbled and deeply plowed" (816). This is an excellent example of the writer testing a maxim's truth, suitability, and usefulness in a particular context: in ultimately arguing that there is no single, absolute interpretation for a text, Montaigne finds Seneca's statement to be true, suitable, and useful to his point. He has brought together his experience and Seneca's insight and tested the truth of the latter in the context of the former.

Wouldn't it be wonderful if our student essayists approached the essays we have them read in the same way? Instead of inserting quotes that have been taken out of context, reduced to isolated entities, and thrust among the students' own essays like fence posts, they might actually test out the truth, the validity, of some essayist's insight. They might meditate on it, try to apply it to some situation in their own lives, bring it into relation with other insights from other essayists and test out the relation between multiple insights when brought into another relationship with some situation. I, for one, would much rather read those essays than the ones where students write what they already think they know, while simultaneously practicing reduction or outright misrepresentation of others' works. After all, how much generation of knowledge, shared discovery, or intellectual exchange are we going to see in writings that do not practice any genuine attentiveness to others—other writers, other ideas, etc.?

THE PROCESS OF UNIFICATION

It's important to remember, though, that in self writing, the writing practices are not simply all about others. They are as much about the subject-that-is-the-writer as about any other author's truth or insight. They are about constituting that subject-that-is-the-writer. To put this in Foucault's terms, "the role of writing is to constitute, along with all that reading has constituted, a 'body.'" That body is constituted because the writing "becomes a principle of rational action in the writer himself." Per this principle, "the writer constitutes his own identity through this recollection of things said" ("Self Writing" 213), unifying these "things said"—the fragments found in his/her *hupomnēmata*—by bringing them together and meditating on them.

To put this in other terms, the writer constitutes his own identity by historicizing his self. Foucault states, "Through the interplay of selected readings and assimilative writing, one should be able to form an identity through which a whole spiritual genealogy can be read" ("Self Writing" 214). To put this in very practical terms, the writer "enters into the conversation," as so many of my colleagues call it, a conversation that may, for example, be between the works of Montaigne and Foucault. In practicing the disparate, the writer becomes a part of the ideas/beliefs s/he is engaged with/in and is remade in them. Consequently, s/he becomes a part of a lineage of ideas, of a system of beliefs, etc.

Thus, an essay is not the transparent representation of an isolated, fixed, stable, "unique" agent, nor is s/he the socially constructed representation of a pre-existing agent in a world that consists of re/oppressive practices. Rather, the self is a historical moment, an event in the movement of discourses. To relay an apt metaphor, Seneca states, "The voices of the individual singers are hidden; what we hear is the voices of all together.... I would have my mind of such a quality as this; it should be equipped with many arts, many precepts, and patterns of conduct taken from many epochs of history; but all should lend harmoniously into one" (qtd. in "Self Writing" 214).

THE SUBJECTED SUBJECT

In reference to classical texts, Foucault states, "The care of the self is the care of the activity and not the care of the soul-as-substance" ("Technologies" 25). In this statement lies the most profound distinction between the technologies of self that are articulated by Foucault and arguably by Montaigne and the writing-of-self described in other versions of subjectivity: the self is not a substance. There is no given, fixed, stable self that is then acted on and manipulated by outside forces. Rather, in the act of writing (an act of caring), selves are constituted. Admittedly, this seeming reversal, where the subject is subjected, flies in the face of most of Western philosophy. In an interview with Foucault, the interviewer states, "But what I don't understand is the position of consciousness as object of an *epistemè*. The consciousness, if anything, is 'epistemizing,' not 'epistemizable'" ("An Historian" 98). This confusion, perhaps, sums up the bewilderment toward Foucault's work on subjectivity, for most of Western philosophy operates within the fundamental belief that "transcendental consciousness... conditions the formation of our knowledge" (98).

The two major theories of subjectivity (what one might call "expressivism" and "social constructionism") in Rhetoric and Composition operate under the assumption that the writer is the agent that can exist outside of its own construction or outside of its social context, even outside of its own mind. Foucault's theory of subjectivity refuses "an equation on the transcendental level between subject and thinking 'I.'" He states, "I am convinced that there exist, if not exactly structures, then at least rules for the functioning of knowledge which have arisen in the course of history and within which can be located the various subjects" ("An Historian" 98). For example, within the *hupomnēmata* there are specific rules—like the (re)reading of other author's texts, like the testing of truths from those texts—that serve as particular operations within which the subject-on-the-page is constituted. Obviously, the writer practices these practices, but s/he is not the transcendent origin of these practices. Rather, the point is that *in* these practices, the self is possible.

To quote Foucault: "[T]hese practices are nevertheless not something invented by the individual himself. They are models that he finds in his culture and are proposed, suggested, imposed upon him by his culture, his society, and his social group" ("The Ethics" 291). Through these models, a relation of self to self is created, and through this relation, selves are constituted differently, newly, so that, for example, the constituted self on the page serves as the material for meditation and transformation of the constituted self of the writer. But, admittedly, it is this conceptual tangle that many scholars may find too alien to engage. So, in the next section, I will unravel this conceptual tangle via a discussion of the care of the self.

CARING FOR THE SELF

Foucault states, "In Greek and Roman texts, the injunction of having to know yourself was always associated with the other principle of having to take care of yourself, and it was that need to care for oneself that brought the Delphic maxim [Know thyself] into operation" ("Technologies" 20). In this, two ideas are most important: through the care of oneself, one knows oneself, and care is not simply a principle but involves a series of practices. Foucault argues that writing was one such practice in caring for oneself. He states, "One of the main features of taking care involved taking notes on oneself to be reread, writing treatises and letters to friends to help them, and keeping notebooks in order to reactivate for oneself the truths one needed" ("Technologies" 27). Examples of these features are evident in Montaigne's works, e.g., where he has written about his endeavors to make a study of himself, to address his dearest friends (see his letter "To the Reader"), and to study other authors' works in order to test the opinions he formed long ago. Examples of these features are also found in the work of Marcus Aurelius. [31] Foucault argues that Marcus Aurelius writes "an example of 'a retreat within oneself': it is a sustained effort in which general principles are reactivated and arguments are adduced that persuade one not to let oneself become angry at others, at providence, or at things" (*Care* 51). [32]

In both cases (of Montaigne's work and in Marcus Aurelius's), the practice of writing is a disciplining of self; it is a way of composing a self that is somehow better—perhaps less angry or fearful of the future. This composing happens because one "retreats into oneself" in the act of caring for oneself, but this does not mean that the writer cares for his/her self by turning inward to examine the essence seated within flesh. Rather, the practices of caring for oneself are ways of producing a subject so that the writer participates in the engineering of the subject, engineering that is a product of knowledge of the production of the subject.

To explain further, I point to a passage from Montaigne in "Of Experience." He states:

> He who calls back to mind the excess of his past anger, and how far this fever carried him away, sees the ugliness of this passion better than in Aristotle, and conceives a more justified hatred for it. He who remembers the evils he has undergone, and those that have threatened him, and the slight causes that have changed him from one state to another, prepares himself in that way for future changes and for recognizing his condition. (822)

In essaying (even in the explanatory excerpt above), Montaigne studies his experiences and assesses his condition; in so doing, a self-on-the-page is constituted, a self that is wiser, less prone to anger, and so on. The ancients knew this kind of writing to be one practice that lends itself to the composition of the self. They practiced this kind of writing in order to participate in the engineering of the self. In that engineering, not only is the self-on-the-page made stronger, but that self serves as material for reflection for the essayist. In meditating on that self, the essayist is transformed, potentially made wiser, etc. This is the self-to-self relation of which I spoke earlier.

That said, if self writing, in general, is done in order to make us better people, then I can foresee essay teachers' and scholars' concerns that I might be condoning the teaching of essay writing as a mode for moralizing students. However, that would be a gross misreading of Foucault's work and of my work here. It would presume, for example, that the practices of self writing should govern a universal self—i.e., that they should objectivize the same type of person, perhaps the moral or civic person—in the same ways and toward the same end. However, for Foucault, self writing is a way of practicing freedom.

By "freedom," Foucault does not necessarily mean "liberation." Rather, he shows that for the Greeks and Romans, "Not to be a slave (of another city, of the people around you, of those governing you, of your own passions) was an absolutely fundamental theme." In turn, "the conscious practice of freedom has revolved around this fundamental imperative: 'Take care of yourself'" ("The Ethics" 285). In this model, where practices (not codes of conduct or morals) are emphasized, "greater attention is paid to the methods, techniques, and exercises directed at forming the self within a nexus of relationships. In such a system, *authority would be self-referential* and might take a therapeutic or philosophical form" (Rabinow xxvii, emphasis added). I am reminded of Socrates saying, "The unexamined life is not worth living." It is this examination that is crucial to the practice(s) of freedom, for in examination, a self is formed—one that does not have to be a slave to the discourses that shape it.

THE SO WHAT AND WHERE TO NOW

This shift in thinking about subjectivity—about how the self is constituted in practices—has implications for how we exchange ideas, how we enter into conversations and participate in them, and most importantly for this project, how we essay. If we took seriously the idea that the subject is constituted in practices, in the practices of self-writing, for example, then we would be able to get past the belief in opinion-as-identity and to actually exchange ideas, share opinions, and, even, potentially cultivate different selves. We'd be able to participate in the generation of other possibilities, in critique, and even (sometimes) in the resolution of conflict—not simply the back-and-forth articulation of what we already know/believe. In other words, *we'd be cultivating more fluid, dynamic selves, not finite selves.*

As such, I could have a productive conversation with the student who joked about the rape of women. I could ask him to examine where his willingness/desire to see humor in violence toward women comes from, where its roots and branches extend and where the shape of that willingness/desire is amplified or diminished. I could ask him to examine, even, why that attitude took hold in him and what it gets him in his work in the care of the self. In other words, I could help him to push his examination of the self-on-the-page further, and with any luck, he'd begin to see that self at play in a complex of discourses of which he, the writer, would also be a part … but differently.

There are at least two major possibilities for essaying and for conceiving of subjectivity in the essay that I'd like readers to take away from this chapter: 1) that essay writing can be discussed and taught according to a series of practices, particularly the practices of meditation (i.e., reading and writing), that it need not rely on a list of conventions; 2) that the relation of the writer to the page is an agonistic one, not a tyrannical or transparent one. The first possibility—that essay writing is a series of practices—stems from the fact that subjectivity does not have to be conceived in terms of an essential or socially constructed self. I have discussed here a different conception of subjectivity, one that is conceived in terms of practices of subjection, and this different conception of subjectivity has implications for how we talk about and teach essays. Instead of talking about and teaching essays as texts that allow students to discover and express their true selves, we might talk about the essay and teach it as a mode that does different kinds of work—work that is still invested in the self, but not The Self (a stable, often hidden, potentially transcendent self).

Regarding the second possibility I'd like readers to take away from this work (that the relation of the writer to the page is not a transparent or tyrannical one), I like to think of the relation, instead, as one of subject to subject— that relation writing me as much as I'm writing the page. As such, even when I receive a critique of this page, I can go into that exchange knowing that this work is not equal to me (and that it is not done). It does not equal who I am, where I come from, or my mind on the page. It's an experiment. A long, arduous, but also in my opinion, compelling and important experiment—one that has made me as much as I have made it.

NOTES

24. Here, I'm deploying a simplistic distinction between voice or the textual self and ethos: the former being the expression/construction of the writer's self on the page (see Chapters 1 and 2) and the latter being the character of the self that is created to establish the writer's credibility and judged according to accepted notions of "the ethical."

25. Here, I'm referring to the concepts that Muckelbauer aligns with the concept (and celebration) of the romantic subject. Within that concept, creativity, originality, and genius all hinge on the belief that the subject is utterly originary—that from it, creation happens. The capacity to create and to exist as the source of creation is "genius."

26. It's important to note that one implication of this different conception of the subject (as one that is subjected) is that this version of subjectivity takes seriously the idea that the writer is one subject being subjected by a number of forces (acting on the body, for example) and that the subject-on-the-page must, therefore, be something different because it is subjected by other forces.

27. Though perhaps obvious, it's worth pointing out that reconceptualizing essay writing as a complex of practices subverts the idea of the innately talented essayist. If we writing teachers want to take seriously the idea that essaying can be taught, then this theory of subjectivity gives us a way to teach it as a complex of practices, as something other than an expressive art that the student writer is inherently "good at" or not.

28. This is not to say that Foucault does not take seriously the question of ownership of texts. In "What is an Author?" his study of the author function does not involve any assumptions about the author-as-creator of the text, though, or about the author-manifested in the text. Rather, Foucault is most interested in the historical operations that are part of the author function, a function that does not invoke the privileging of an author's agency over/in a text, but is an enunciation of how the author's name provides a mode of "existence, circulation, and functioning of certain

discourses" (211). For example, a text with the name "Montaigne" attached to it can be expected to be a prototype of the essay. It can be expected to be written in a meandering, contemplative mode; to quote many important, classical authors; to incorporate personal experiences; and to be relentlessly skeptical of its own claims.

29. The similarities here in Foucault's articulation of self writing and Montaigne's description of being made by his book are very likely due, at least in part, to the fact that Montaigne was such an avid reader of Seneca's work—a writer who was very much invested in the self-disciplining practices of self writing. Montaigne goes so far as to write about the "Seneca in [him]" in his essay "Of Books" (297), and in the same essay, he states that the books from which he learned "to arrange [his] humors and [his] ways" are those of Plutarch and Seneca (it's worth noting, too, that in the 2003 Penguin Edition of Montaigne's essays, translator M.A. Screech uses the verb "control," instead of "arrange" (463)).

As Foucault points out, "[...T]he theme of application of oneself to oneself is well known [in Antiquity]: it is to this activity… that a man must devote himself, to the exclusion of other occupations" (*Care* 46). Montaigne, too, takes this occupation as seriously as the writers of Antiquity. He states, "For those who go over themselves in their minds and occasionally in speech do not penetrate to essentials in their examination as does a man who makes that his study, his work, and his trade, who binds himself to keep an enduring account, with all his faith, with all his strength" ("Of Giving" 504). I should note that "essentials," as Montaigne is using the term, refers to tendencies or habits, not to an essence of self.

30. In "On Keeping a Notebook," Didion argues that we should use our notebooks to "keep in touch" with old selves, past experiences, seemingly fleeting ideas/images/feelings. She states, "It is a good idea, then, to keep in touch, and I suppose that keeping in touch is what notebooks are all about" (140).

31. Though I've not found any evidence of the claim in my own reading, Bensmaïa states in *The Barthes Effect* that Marcus Aurelius's *Meditations* is one of the models that have been "invoked" as a "springboard" for the essay (90). In general, the essay scholarship I've read that reaches for roots older than Montaigne's essays most often points to Seneca (see Lopate and Hall, for example).

32. Incidentally, this phrase "a retreat within oneself" should sound very familiar to Montaigne/essay scholars, for it is commonly used (even by him) to describe his work.

CHAPTER 4: IMITATION AS MEDITATION

> Those who do not want to imitate anything, produce nothing.
>
> -Salvador Dali

On the first day of my first undergraduate creative writing class, I sat in the back of the room and listened to the whispered anticipation and fear from those who would soon be my writing-competitors, as we waited for our famous poet-teacher to make her first appearance. When she finally walked in, we all stared, rapt as this surprisingly small woman crossed to the front of the classroom and began to pace before the board.

Over the next fifteen weeks, she gave us sentences from her favorite novels to write from; she played opera sung by her favorite soprano and cried while we listened; she talked of inspiration and voice and of the silencing and oppressive acts of the white man and of popular culture; she said that the things we love—music, writing, people—have heartbeats that jive with our own; she quoted James Whitmore saying, "I'm not qualified to teach you, but I can pass on to you what I've learned"; and she gave me an "ok" on my in-class writings with no other comments until my final project—a collection of poems—on which she wrote "Fantastic! A" with no other margin or end comments.

There were at least a couple of exceptions in my studies (e.g., a creative nonfiction professor in my MA program who commented at length and at different stages of the writing process on my work), but for the most part, I found that my creative writing courses all went the same way: the teachers told us about the ideas/images/music, etc., that inspired them; they gave us examples of good creative writing; and they commented very little, if at all, on the content of our works. No doubt, there are many other exceptions to the course I've just described. After my coursework as a creative writing student, however, I was left wondering if my experience in receiving little in the way of written feedback was a too-common practice in such courses. I have never found a definitive answer, but the question stayed with me, as I went on to become a writing teacher and a writing program administrator.

When I first served as an English department's composition director and read the instructors' comments to the personal essays that some assigned in their first-year writing courses, I saw much less commenting on those papers than I did on others—a problem I attributed, at the time, to composition teachers not knowing the genre well enough to make substantial comments. However, even now, when I serve with creative writing professors on creative-writing-focused thesis committees, I find that even their comments on content are broad and sparse and that, at some point, the question of the student's talent (the presumably innate capacity to write well) comes up.

Again, this is not to suggest that all teachers of creative nonfiction neglect offering extensive feedback to their students' works. Such an assertion seems ludicrous. Rather, I'm more interested in common practices—in students' more typical experiences in such courses. This is also not to suggest that teachers of creative nonfiction, even those who don't offer much in the way of written comments, don't know how to teach writing. On the contrary, my first creative writing teacher and her stories about what personally inspired her got me to pay more attention—e.g., to what inspired me, to what seemed to evoke emotion in others, to how the trivial might serve as a powerful metaphor for the immense, and to how being moved felt better than any other experience I'd known. On the other hand, after four years of study and practice in creative nonfiction, I still had no articulable way of describing what my writing was like and really only knew intuitively what worked and what didn't work in my writing. All I knew for sure was that for some reason that generally had something to do with my passion or my voice or my style—compliments that I appreciated but only vaguely understood—a few creative writing teachers liked my personal essays.

I've seen evidence of the same in my creative nonfiction students' experiences, too, and across three different universities where I have worked. For example, today, in an online class discussion forum within an introductory-level personal essay course, a student shared with the class the fact that though her writing teachers talked about her voice in her creative and personal writings in grade school, she never actually saw "voice" defined. At least a handful of her classmates agreed, saying they had the same experience. I asked the group to explain how they understood their prior teachers' comments on voice, and I got a variety of answers—from "the teacher was talking about my personality" to "the teacher liked my writing style" and so on. All agreed that, really, they didn't have a clear sense of what the comments meant.

This confusion and lack of specificity does not seem to occur only in regard to comments about voice. In my Ph.D. program, when I was teaching a course on the personal essay, I had a student who had been writing personal essays for several years and sharing them with various audiences. She'd generally gotten positive responses to her work, as readers consistently told her that her writing seemed "smart" and "different." After we read her first essay in class, I jokingly called her "The Metaphor Queen," and in response she exclaimed, "That's it! That's what they mean! No one ever put it like that before." In what was for me an alarming moment, it became clear that no one had ever told her that what made her personal essays smart and surprising—and at times, confusing and unwieldy—was her prolific use of metaphor. Unfortunately, I could easily recount many similar examples of students not being able to identify the tendencies, habits, strengths, and weaknesses in their creative nonfiction writing.

This probably seems, at first, odd (it did to me). One might think that in my own case and in my students', perhaps we'd had poor or sloppy readers in the past. But, it seems to me that we had very good readers—good, at least, at encouraging us to continue writing, and perhaps that is the point. This suggests, though, one of two (if not both of the following) assumptions: 1. students will become stronger creative nonfiction writers simply by writing frequently; and 2. creative nonfiction writing doesn't need much written feedback.[33] Perhaps it's no surprise, but both of these assumptions align perfectly with Elbow's early work on voice. In *Writing with Power*, Elbow says that he had his students write "15 pages a week" and admits that he read their work "quickly and intermittently" (282), commenting very little on each piece. His purpose: to discover voice in writing. I often wonder how thoroughly creative nonfiction teachers have inherited and come to practice the same, and with the same purpose in mind.[34]

When I consider my own and my students' experiences, I wonder how many of our teachers were responding to our texts as if they were extensions of our selves (e.g., in the claim that my personal essays embodied my "passion"). If I'm right, if creative nonfiction teachers tend to see the essay as an expression of the writer's mind on the page, then perhaps that is why there is a lack of specificity in their comments. All the writer would need to learn to express his/her mind are more chances to do exactly that and maybe a little help with form and style to make that expression more powerful.

Again, if I'm right, then these assumptions and their attendant practices reflect, certainly, the version of subjectivity described in Chapter 1. However, they also work within the version of subjectivity described in Chapter 2, for even in an essay that takes seriously the concept of the self as a socially constructed entity, that entity's construction on the page is still believed to be a re-presentation of the self of the flesh and blood writer. In fact, as shown in Chapter 2, readers (like Pratt) make assumptions about and comment on the living writer based on the "evidence" about his/her life, experiences, thoughts, values, etc., that are articulated on the page. If one teaches essay writing within either version of subjectivity, then the essay becomes an exercise in discovering how to accurately and effectively express or re-present the self on the page.

Interestingly (when considered in relation to the sparse commenting creative nonfiction teachers often give), essay textbooks generally offer little, if any, instruction to help students do the work of re-presenting the self.[35] For example, two well-received and popular essay textbooks are Robert L. Root and Michael Steinberg's *The Fourth Genre* and Phillip Lopate's *The Art of the Personal Essay*. Both are anthologies in the strictest sense, with the first focusing on various subgenres of creative nonfiction and the second focusing specifically on the personal essay. Each text includes a rather lengthy introduction that makes some attempt at defining the genre, pointing out some of its conventions, and discussing what's interesting about the genre as well as what's difficult about it. Beyond the introduction, the only commentary from Lopate is in the biographies included before each text (again, suggesting that to read an essay one should know something of the writer); Root and Steinberg only include short (roughly a page and a half of text) introductions to the three major sections of the textbook. To my mind, the lack of instruction in anthologies and their prevalence suggest that students are expected to learn to write essays via imitation.

Though this is not necessarily explicitly explained in essay anthologies, the assumption seems to be that students learn to write successful essays by studying how the master essayists did it—not by studying the masters' writing processes, per se, but by examining the essays produced by these master essayists and exploring the ways in which they responded to the events/materials/people presented to them in their lives. I am reminded, for example, of the famous, small-statured writing teacher of my first creative writing course, who shared with us the pieces of music and literature that had inspired her to write some of her best works.

Of course, studying the masters' works in order to improve one's own work is, by no means, a new method for invention; its roots trace back more than two thousand years, and as a pedagogical method, it appears with great force (and contention) throughout the rhetorical tradition. That said, per the most common conception of subjectivity in the essay (articulated in the first chapter of this project), imitation seems, at first, to be an ill-suited strategy for essay writing. If the essay is an expression of the essential self of the essayist, then how does my imitation of F. Scott Fitzgerald's voice, for example, give me access to my own? Or, in the context of the socially constructed self, how would imitating his voice help me to construct my own—given that mine occurs in a vastly different context and would be constructed from vastly different social categories (e.g., female, academic, sister, etc.)? By extension, it also seems strange that there are few essay textbooks with exercises asking students to plumb their innerness or to examine their "constructedness" and to voice that innerness or constructedness in different kinds of ways. All of these points leave us with the question: why imitation? *How* is imitation supposed to get students access to the true self or the constructed self so that they can render this self on the page authentically?

Given my work in prior chapters to establish and explore connections between the essay (as a tradition, practice, and genre) to the scholarship and pedagogical insights of rhetoric and composition scholars and teachers, I will in this chapter explore the history of imitative pedagogy in the rhetorical tradition, as well as in composition pedagogy; in doing so, I will address, first, the seeming contradiction at work in a pedagogy (re)produced for a genre invested in and driven by the close relationship between the self-on-the-page and its unique writer.

IMITATION AS A PRACTICE OF HOMOGENIZATION

According to composition scholar Frank D'Angelo in his 1973 *College Composition and Communication* article "Imitation and Style," imitation should be understood as "the process whereby the writer participates not in stereotypes, but in archetypal forms and ideas" (283). This emphasis on "archetypal forms and ideas" should sound familiar to essay scholars and teachers, given that one of the emphases in discussions on the essay is its participation in universal truths, and in this emphasis, the pedagogical use of imitation certainly seems justified. For example, in Lopate's Introduction to *The Art of the Personal Essay*, he states, "At the core of the personal essay is the supposition that there is a certain unity to human experience. As Michel de Montaigne ... put it, 'Every man has within himself the entire human condition.' This meant that when he was telling about himself, he was talking, to some degree, about all of us" (xxiii). In this particular reading of Montaigne, one finds an Expressivist sentiment: that the individual's truths mirror everyone else's. The renowned rhetoric and composition scholar, James Berlin explains, "The underlying conviction of expressionists is that when individuals are spared the distorting effects of a repressive social order, their privately determined truths will correspond to the privately corresponding truths of all others" (486). It follows, then, that if the essay is the genuine, unfiltered, personal expression of the writer's self and his truths, which necessarily correspond to others' truths, then imitating Fitzgerald's essays may actually grant me access to my own truths.

One could easily get bogged down here in the dangerous assumption that my truth, for example, should correspond to that of an African American male who lived and wrote in the 1950s, or that it could correspond to that of a prepubescent female, one who lived in the 1980s in the former Soviet Union. Many scholars in Rhetoric and Composition have pointed to this danger in their scholarship (see Bizzell's description of "the turn to the social" in "Foundationalism and Anti-foundationalism"). As such, I think it's safe to assume that any writing teacher working today would hesitate to teach "universals" or "human nature." Too, in most contemporary personal essays (see, for example, Barbara Kingsolver's "Household Words," Lawrence Gonzales's "Marion Prison," or Demetria Martinez's "Inherit the Earth" and "The Things They Carried"), essayists now do this "universalizing" not by actually speaking for the whole of humanity but by trying to speak to an issue that is bigger than his/her self. For example, in "Household Words," Kingsolver begins the essay with a story about her driving home one day and witnessing an assault. However, the essay quickly moves from her personal experience to the much larger issue of homelessness in America.

I could offer Kingsolver's essay to my students as an example of "how to speak to the bigger issues," and I think they would be receptive to reading it as such. However, given the three major conventions of the essay (see Chapter 1), if I were to ask them, then, to write an essay in which they must imitate the way Kingsolver structures her essay, they would, no doubt, find the exercise disingenuous—because it would prevent the student from producing a true essay, e.g., one that utilizes the freedom and "natural" way of expressing the writer's mind that is key to any essay. In the conception of the socially constructed self that I've explained in Chapter 2, given the importance of context, it seems counterintuitive to suggest that imitating Kingsolver's essay (which would constitute a form of contextualization) would provide an effective way of constructing their own self-on-the-page. Rather, it would be exceedingly easy to assume that in imitating another's way of re-presenting the self, one risks conformity and uniformity—two qualities that would be kryptonite to the power of the personal essay.

I see this assumption about imitation, as well as a more complex relationship to it, most clearly when discussing the institutionalization of Standard English with students. In such conversations, students often make this argument: in order to understand, to be understood—to be part of a discourse community—they must use a common language and common language conventions. No doubt, as I've shown in Chapter 1, the essay works in a similar way: for a text to be recognized as an essay, it must embody the conventions that constitute the genre. Inevitably, though, my students begin to get uncomfortable when terms like "diversity" and "homogeneity" are introduced in the same conversation. They, like many writing teachers, find an emphasis on imitating convention in any discourse and in any text to be suspect, if not counter-productive to the student's development as an autonomous thinker (and writer).

Common conceptions of imitation suggest that it is a homogenizing practice, which if carried to its end, would make us like a series of holograms—shadows of the same model, a kind of one-dimensional reflection of something/someone more substantial. In tracing a history of imitation in writing pedagogy, Bob Connors argues that the romanticism of the 1970s, in particular, is responsible for the devaluing, if not rejection, of the practices of imitation in the writing classroom. He states, "The romanticism of the age … would grow more and more potent as the 1970s segued into the 1980s. Teachers and theorists reacted against any form of practice that seemed to compromise originality and the expression of personal feelings, and imitation exercises were among the most obvious indoctrinations to 'tradition' and 'the system'" (467). This indoctrination seemed to be the inevitable consequence of imitation exercises that were "context-stripped from what students really wanted to say themselves" (Connors 468). In other words, it was believed that the exercises made students automatons—parrots, if you will, of the model text/author—instead of active learners and participants in a discourse, where what they intended to say should have been the most important factor in their learning and participation. Consequently, writing teachers, along with their writing students, became disenchanted with imitation exercises and talked, instead, about a learning process that many believed imitation exercises would not accommodate.

For example, in his book titled *Teaching the Universe of Discourse* (1968), James Moffett states, "I would not ask a student to write anything other than an *authentic* discourse, because the learning process proceeds from intent and content down to the contemplation of technical points [the latter of which was taught through imitation exercises], not the other way" (205, emphasis added). The term "authentic," when used to describe a writer's work, typically suggests that the expression originates in and from the writer (from his/her intention), not from convention, and that the writer's intentions, including his/her intended meaning, are most important—trumping, even, the writer's skill and deployment of conventions in writing.

This conception of authentic writing, too, hinges on a belief that language is a transparent vehicle (driven by the writer, of course) for the expression of the writer (his/her mind and intentions) on the page—the very same concept of language explored at length in Chapter 1, in the conception of the essential self expressed on the page. As demonstrated in Chapter 1, the problems proliferate in this conception: it is to blame for the seeming risk one takes in using imitation to learn the essay, for example. Indeed, I only risk homogenization if language is, in fact, just a vehicle for the expression (or construction) of the self; only then does my imitation of Fitzgerald's essay mean that I am, essentially, imitating his self on the page, re-presenting it as if it were my own.

However, though the use of imitation may have its problems within conceptions of the essential and the socially constructed self on the page, it provides writers with interesting and effective possibilities for studying and practicing the essay within the version of subjectivity described in Chapter 3. Thus, to put this really simply: there's no need to throw the baby out with the bathwater. All we, as essay teachers, scholars, and writers need is a bit of reorientation to the practice, a reorientation that is ultimately a return to older uses of imitation.

Chapter Four

A DIFFERENT CONCEPTION OF IMITATION

As has been argued and demonstrated at length in Chapter 3, any subject that is revealed on the page is not actually the same as that of the flesh-and-blood writer; rather, the two subjects work and are (re)constituted in relation to one another. Consequently, the use of imitation as part of an essay pedagogy shifts, for if the self on the page and the self of the writer are different subjects, constituted differently, then imitation does not enable the cloning effect that so many writers worry about; rather, variety is inevitable. To explain this seeming contradiction, I'll have to explain a very different concept of originality, first.

Unlike common conceptions of originality—that it stems from some unfiltered, untainted part (the essence) of a writer—the concept of originality for which I'd like to advocate is one where originality stems, instead, from a "happening" within a discourse. I, like William Gruber, would argue that there is no originality without the writer having "a defined area to work in" (497): namely, the feared and, consequently, avoided "tradition" or "system." To carry this idea at least a few steps further, I'd argue that when students imitate, when they participate in the practices of imitation, they are not only discovering effective ways of essaying. They are, in fact, participating in discourse (or multiple discourses), establishing their work within contexts and traditions that give the work ground—both to root itself in and from which to push off. Though they may not be constructing an "authentic" discourse in the way Moffett means it (a discourse that originates in, from, and becomes the expression of the unique and autonomous subject that is the writer), they are ultimately participating in the constituting of a self in discourse—and not a self that is merely a carbon copy of some other self.

As I've shown in Chapter 3, one way that the Ancients (and Montaigne) worked to constitute a self in discourse was through the care of the self, of which the practices of self writing were a part. Within those self writing practices, the *hupomnēmata*, a category within which I have placed the essay, served as materials for meditation (easily the primary practice in self writing). In self writing, however, meditation does not involve plumbing one's innerness and reflecting on it. As Foucault states, "The intent is not to pursue the unspeakable, nor to reveal the hidden, nor to say the unsaid, but on the contrary to capture the already-said, to collect what one has managed to hear or read, and for the purpose that is nothing less than the shaping of the self" ("Self Writing" 210-211). To put this simply, in the practices of self writing, writers collect what they've read, explore the connections and contradictions they see among the parts, and they try to piece them all together. They are not necessarily looking for some consistent truth, but they are considering relations, making sense of connections and ruptures. We scholars already know this process, for we spend our days reading immense amounts of material, considering it, and in the meditative act of writing, we try to "make sense" of it: we try to thread it together in such a way that parts speak to/with each other like singers in a chorus.

Extending this metaphor a little further, the music produced in that chorus is a result of the process of "unification," and according to Foucault, said unification occurs *in the self*. Foucault states, "But [unification] is not implemented in the art of composing an ensemble; it must be established in the writer himself, as a result of the *hupomnēmata*, of their construction (and hence in the very act of writing) and of their consultation (and hence in their reading and rereading)" ("Self Writing" 213). In order for unification to be established in the writer, Foucault argues, quoting Seneca (and, likely, Nietzsche), that we must "digest" the material, through the processes of reading and writing. In fact, Seneca goes so far as to say that "We should see to it that whatever we have absorbed should not be allowed to remain unchanged, or it will be not part of us. We must digest it" (qtd in Foucault "Self Writing" 213).

Here, one can see the fundamentally different conception of subjectivity at work in the care of the self and, hopefully, the radical change to conceptions of imitation and, thus, to originality: we do not simply encounter ideas, perspectives, and/or evidence and then force them into a discernable pattern or image, like a puzzle-master might; rather, we must "digest" material in order for it to become a part of us. Foucault states, "It is one's own soul that must be constituted in what one writes; but, just as a man bears his natural resemblance to his ancestors on his face, so it is good that one can perceive the filiation of thoughts that are engraved *in* his soul" ("Self Writing" 214, emphasis added). Foucault does not say engraved "on" his soul; he says "in." This distinction is important, for in it, one can see that the self is constituted in practices, e.g., of self writing, and that the self (or soul) that occurs at any moment is genealogical in nature; it is not essential, not socially-constructed, but inherited; it is the moment of absorption, of integration.

Foucault is not describing a self that is stable, pre-social, transcendent. He is not describing a self that is determined by distinct social categories, e.g. race, gender, sexuality, etc. He's describing a self that is utterly historical and also momentary—a self that is constituted in practices in which writers can participate, but that do not originate in writers; a self that is the momentary collision of so many ideas, beliefs, perspectives, but is not the creator of all of those ideas, beliefs, perspectives; a self that is conditional, shifting, indefinite, and a product of the discourses that are already, always at work; a self that happens, that is a "happening," within those discourses.

If we buy this different conception of the self, then the question that follows

Chapter Four

is always about how the writer participates in his/her own constituting: how does s/he *do* anything, create anything? Where is originality in this relation? To answer these questions, in thinking about this process of constituting the self by reading and capturing-through-writing the already-said, I want to direct our attention to how one's thinking and writing are constituted in an encounter with a text, specifically when that text serves as a model to be imitated.

Take, for example, Seneca's metaphor of bees gathering honey:

> We also, I say, ought to *copy* these bees, and sift whatever we have gathered from a varied course of reading [...]; then, by applying the supervising *care* with which our nature has endowed us [...], we should so blend those several flavours into one delicious compound that, even though it betrays its origin, yet it nevertheless is clearly *a different thing from that whence it came*. [...] We must digest [this material]; otherwise it will merely enter the memory and not the reasoning power. [...] This is what our mind should do: it should hide away all the materials by which it has been aided, and bring to light only *what it has made of them*. Even if there shall appear in you a likeness to him who, by reason of your admiration, has left a deep impress upon you, I would have you resemble him as a child resembles his father, and *not* as a picture resembles its original [...]. (279-281, emphasis added)

Seneca calls us to copy the bees, to imitate their behavior, or in the terms of self writing, to imitate a practice: i.e., to gather material. The "gathering" of material and the "blending" of it is the reading and rereading and writing about that material in order to bring it into our minds and make something of it, to produce thought, insight, and other material which can, in turn, be digested again by others (and by the self).

The digestive process, then, works on at least a couple of levels: it occurs when the writer reads, again when the writer writes, and again when the writer reads what s/he is writing. These "levels" are so difficult to separate out, in fact, that the term "levels" fails to capture the process, yet I struggle to come up with another term. My point, though, is that one is not ever simply receiving information in some passive state when s/he writes or reads, not even when s/he writes or reads to imitate. The activity of engaging with a text is more complicated than any theory of language-transmitting-knowledge suggests. Because there is no simple route for transmission (from writer to word to reader), originality is more complicated, too.

If knowledge (including self-knowledge) is not transmitted but is generated, is sustained/created, in the encounter between writer and text and reader, then originality of thought, for example, is not some quality transmitted from writer to page. Rather, originality of thought is a quality that is experienced because of the inevitable variety that occurs in the encounter between writer and text and reader and text and so on. I explain it to my students this way: innumerable forces are working in me (time, gravity, etc.), and those forces are made sense of within various discourses (e.g., of ethnicity and age and gender, etc.), and all of those relations that for a brief moment constitute a "me" are brought into relation with, say, Montaigne's "Of Experience." Something happens in that encounter; no doubt, many somethings happen—too many to account for in a stable, consistent "me."

At first, my students find this different conception of subjectivity to be overwhelming, sometimes infuriating. But, eventually, many of them recognize and embrace the fact that in this different conception of subjectivity, a different kind of subject emerges—one that is not "given" by Nature or by a society, but one that is constituted in forces and discourses and can, thus, not only change but be changed. In other words, my students begin to see that who they are is not determined, and then, with the help of a few models, they begin to feel some hope for participating in their own constitution. That is when I bring in model texts that investigate the self and in which the writer works to participate in his/her own constitution—not those who look for who they are at some essential core or who they are determined to be by social forces. Rather, I introduce them to writers who "broke the mold" in working to know the self. For all that his work is despised and misunderstood, Nietzsche's longer works are excellent examples of a writer participating in his own constitution by digesting the "already said."

For example, here's how Nietzsche "inherits," or digests and makes something of, Seneca's bee metaphor in *Genealogy of Morals*: "It has rightly been said: 'Where your treasure is, there will your heart be also'; our treasure is where the beehives of our knowledge are. We are constantly making for them, being by nature winged creatures and honey-gatherers of the spirit; there is one thing alone we really care about from the heart—'bringing something home'" (15). In this metaphor, beehives are where the production of knowledge happens. And, according to Nietzsche, we are always striving for those sites of production. We are always working to return to the hive, to recognize what we've discovered, to see how we know, to digest our inventions and the inventions of others, and to render the unified body that is (self)knowledge.

In self writing, one is able to do exactly that: the writer meditates on material in order to digest it, to do something with it, to know it, and in knowing and digesting and doing, to constitute a self. As Foucault explains, "The role of writing is to constitute, along with all that reading has constituted, a 'body' [that which digests and can be digested]" ("Self Writing" 213). This body can be the body of the book, the material work, the material production. As scholars, we recognize this process every time we say something like, "Nietzsche is…," according to the body that is constituted in his published works.

How is this moment of recognition, though, different from the one that Pratt describes in "Arts of the Contact Zone," where she describes Poma-the-author as equal to the same collection of social, historical, and political elements that make up Poma-the-man? It is different because in the process of self writing, i.e., in the processes of meditation, and in the recognition of how those processes work, when we say "Nietzsche," we acknowledge that we cannot capture the flesh-and-blood figure; we can only refer to the body that is his work. That said, we can also acknowledge that in engaging with the text that is "Nietzsche," we are engaging with a text that helped to shape the flesh-and-blood man. Somehow, that is an incredibly powerful realization—perhaps more powerful than the assumption that his text is simply a reflection of his original self.

NIETZSCHE'S MEDITATIONS ON MONTAIGNE

I say that this realization is powerful, in part, simply because Nietzsche so deliberately, even obsessively, meditated on Montaigne's work.[36] As a result, both writers, though two very different writers, seem to have been working on the same project—what it might mean to know the self and how to go about knowing it. In their efforts, both recognized and discussed at length the same obstacle to that project (our obsession with the future). And, both attempted to work through that obstacle in the same meditative form (the essay) and within the same meditative practices found in self writing (e.g., the truth test). What ends up on the page of one writer, though, looks very different from the other.

In his introduction to the reader, Montaigne states that he has written this book of essays for his friends and family, "so that when they have lost me (as soon they must), they may recover here some features of my habits and temperament, and by this means keep the knowledge they have had of me more complete and alive." He goes on to say that he has tried to portray his self simply, "without straining or artifice." In the end of the address, he states, "Thus, reader, I am myself the matter of my book" (2). To summarize, then, Montaigne tells his reader that he has made his self the subject of his collection of essays in order to grant his reader the material with which they could "recover" some features of him. He does not say, "here I am." Rather, he says that his self is the material, the subject, of the book. And, this distinction is interesting because it suggests, again, that the text produced is a constituted body, rendered in a series of meditations that can, in turn, be meditated on by others—which is exactly what Nietzsche did.

One can see the intensity of Montaigne's project's influence on Nietzsche's own project in the Preface to *On the Genealogy of Morals*. Nietzsche begins the text with this: "We are unknown to ourselves, we men of knowledge [...]." A few lines later, he continues:

> Present experience has, I am afraid, always found us 'absent-minded': we cannot give our hearts to it—not even our ears! Rather, as one divinely preoccupied and immersed in himself into whose ear the bell has just boomed with all its strength the twelve beats of noon suddenly starts up and asks himself; 'what really was that which just struck?' so we sometimes rub our ears afterward and ask, utterly surprised and disconcerted, 'what really was that which we have just experienced?' and moreover: 'who are we really?' and, afterward as aforesaid, count the twelve trembling bell-strokes of our experience, our life, our being—and alas! Miscount them.—so we are necessarily strangers to ourselves [...]. We are not 'men of knowledge' with respect to ourselves. (15)

I quote this extensive passage because I think it an excellent example of the essayistic (or explorative) development of ideas that Nietzsche is so famous for—i.e., the way in which he develops an idea by mapping back over content and intensifying it with each new sentence. More importantly, this passage demonstrates that, as he develops the analogy of the man startled by the clock's bell, Nietzsche introduces his project. In the larger text, he will explore just who and what we are, or more specifically, how we came to be who and what we are. Part of that "how" is a consequence of our practice of negation of present experience, our rejection of it, as we obsess, instead, over the future. In the end, Nietzsche will argue that man is a sick animal because of that negation, because he is "eternally directed toward the future." Nietzsche states that man's "restless energies never leave him in peace, so that his future digs like a spur into the flesh of every present" (121). It is a compelling metaphor—one that stands, in part, for the god-fearing man living for the afterlife, the ultimate future, and a future that, in turn, requires him to negate the value of this life, except as a means to the greater end.

Montaigne, on the other hand, seems not to be obsessed with that "ultimate" future; rather, he cares to make himself strong, resilient for any future strife in this life, as I've shown in Chapter 3. He finds, though, that sacrificing the present for worry about any future is dangerous. In fact, he quotes Seneca, who warns that such worry makes us "vulnerable." In "Our Feelings Reach Out Beyond Us," Montaigne states, "We are never at home, we are always beyond. Fear, desire, hope, project us toward the future and steal from us the feeling and consideration of what is, to busy us with what will be, even when we shall no longer be. 'A soul anxious about the future is most vulnerable'" (8). This insight may very well be that which inspired Nietzsche's *On the Genealogy of Morals*, for the book is, arguably, a response to this very insight. Nietzsche says as much in the Preface, as the passage above demonstrates.

Perhaps, then, it is not too much of a stretch to argue that Nietzsche's collection of essays (*On the Genealogy of Morals*) is a meditation on our obsession with the future and what it has done to shape the genealogy of Western morality. Through that insight and meditation, his work has emerged as uniquely Nietzschean, though so obviously (to me, at least) grounded in, driven by, the works of his genealogical predecessor, Montaigne. Most importantly, I see a model in this relation between Montaigne's and Nietzsche's work—one that could have game-changing pay-offs for our essay students today.

FOR OUR STUDENTS

I recommend that we, as essay teachers, frame our essay classes around the practices of the "care of self," as I've described here and in Chapter 3. Unlike more typical essay classes, then, this change would mean that we not simply ask them to read essays and come to class ready to talk about them, that we not simply ask them to write essays and come to class ready to share them. If students are to learn how to write meditative essays, then they must learn by practice, but not just any practice, certainly not just by writing *more*. Rather, as I've shown, there are specific practices available to them that are graspable, doable, and void of scary and/or inaccessible requests, such as "find your true voice" or "reconstruct your self in a socially critical way." The practices of imitation in an essay classroom should operate like practices of meditation: they should encourage students to read, reread, to engage, reengage, to write, rewrite in response to the essays they've read, to the conversations they've participated in, to what they see, hear, think day to day.

After all, we are not writing in a vacuum. When writing, we are always participating in discourses, always practicing the (writing/speaking) practices that are already available to us; however, by participating in the constellation of discourses and practices that are at work in a particular movement, in a particular stroke of pen on page or finger on keyboard, we are always doing something *different* with what's been done before—even and especially when participating in the practices of imitation-as-meditation. If we really intensify those practices, then I believe our students will produce much meatier essays, essays that are inevitably different and self-constituting because of the intensity of the meditation.

This seems to me to be one of many options for introducing students to a method of essaying via imitation that is productive. Student essayists can practice the essay by meditating on the issues, insights, and strategies explored by other essayists in other essays; their imitation, though, would be less about mimicking content or technique and more about starting somewhere. They can start by answering the claim of another text, examining it at length within its own context and in other contexts (think about the "truth test" described in Chapter 3). The key is in the examination—what I've been calling "meditation." It is, perhaps, a circular process, one in which insights are "digested" (ingested and re-produced differently), but in that process, the student recognizes that insights do not occur "out of the blue" and that the self, too, does not occur from spontaneous generation. In such ways, essaying would become something other than simply navel-gazing. It would be a practice that requires intense study, used for the purpose of constituting a self on the page that can in turn be used as material for study.

Students may come to know their selves in essaying, but certainly not a fixed self, certainly not a stable self. They would begin to see the self as, yes, continuous, but not as entirely consistent. They would begin to see that the self on the page changes, not only because of their own changes of mood and experience, but because of what they've read, the shape of the assignment, the demands of their reader/grader, the experimental grammar used in an essay, the skepticism practiced in it, and so on and on. They would recognize, too, that the self that is constituted, then, on the page is not somehow "less true" because it is constituted within these contours, but is possible because of these contours, which brings us to the focus of the next chapter: how to set up such contours in order to enable this kind of essaying in an essay course.

NOTES

33. Perhaps the lack of specificity in readings of student writing practices/strategies in personal essays is due, in part, to the fact that, as Lynn Bloom notes in "The Essay Canon," there is not enough critical work in response to essays (403)—scholarly readings that might serve as models for in-the-classroom readings.

34. Please note that Elbow does not in any of his works claim that writing teachers should comment little on their students' works. As I've shown elsewhere, he does value and call for feedback for student writing. Perhaps he isn't commenting much on student writing at this early point in his career (when *Writing Without Teachers*

Chapter Four

and *Writing with Power* were published) because he hasn't fully figured out what writing with voice is yet—and thus, how to comment on it. Unfortunately, I think that writing teachers have inherited this idea that they don't need to comment much on student writing, at least not if they are most interested in identifying where voice seems to occur in the text and where it doesn't.

35. I have found that when the essay is included in composition textbooks, there is more instructional material incorporated. For example, in *The Allyn and Bacon Guide to Writing* (3rd ed), Ramage, et al., talk at greater lengths about the essay's emphasis on exploration and provide exercises for exploration. I've also found, though, that the essay is used in composition textbooks as a kind of preliminary writing tool for the more serious stuff of arguments (like in the case of *The Allyn and Bacon Guide*). The textbooks that take the essay more seriously, as a genre worth studying and practicing in its own right (not toward another end), are generally creative nonfiction anthologies. In my project here, though, I don't want to denigrate the personal essay to a mere brainstorming-exercise, nor do I want to accept the practice of teaching-via-anthology at face value.

36. It's well-recognized that Nietzsche was an avid reader of Montaigne's works. For specifics, see Dorothea Heitsche's "Nietzsche and Montaigne: Concepts of Style." In it, Heitsch lists the various accounts of Nietzsche talking in letters and in notes about reading Montaigne's *Essais*. Heitsche also notes, though, that little had been said of the relationship between the two writers, as of the publication of her article (1999), and I'd argue that there is still a disappointing lack of treatment of that relationship in scholarship in Rhetoric and Composition and in Creative Confiction.

CHAPTER 5: SELF WRITING IN THE CLASSROOM

I think any experienced instructor or professor recognizes a rigorous course, when s/he teaches one. On the other hand, what counts as rigorous to our students may be different from what counts as such to us. After more than a decade teaching, I am still surprised, for example, when I receive student evaluations for a couple of my lower-level writing courses that laud the depth of class discussions—especially given that I still find the work we do in those courses to be stilted and frustrating, as I struggle to accurately assess and to push my students' engagement in them. Consequently, for my part, I think it wise to have taught a few upper-level courses in self writing before introducing the concept in a lower-level writing course. That way, you can figure out where you're going, so to speak, in the larger writing curriculum, what you want students to be able to manage in a captstone self writing course, and you can work back from there to help them to that end. For example, after trying out self writing twice in upper level creative nonfiction courses (a 300-level and a 400-level), I began teaching a unit of self writing, using primarily the works of Seneca as models, in our introductory-level personal essay course. I found that at least a few students in the course seemed to "get it" and were invested in the practices; in fact, they continued with the curriculum. For the purposes of this chapter, however, I am offering insights about, a framework for, teaching materials for, and student essays from upper-level personal essay courses that center in the practices of self writing almost exclusively.

Obviously, the two most important practices in a self writing course are reading and writing. Both practices, though, must enable meditation—not simply reading for content or writing to argue for a particular interpretation of a text or for a particular perspective on an issue. Again, this is one of the reasons why an upper-level course in self writing works well: by the time they take the course, students have likely already progressed in their reading capabilities beyond the practice of simply reading for comprehension. Too, I find that I don't have to sell them on the value of writing-to-explore an idea. They are generally open to, excited about, the prospect of writing-to-explore, instead of writing-to-argue. My job, then, becomes one of raising their awareness of the reading and writing practices they already participate in, amplifying any meditative practices that might work in those reading/writing practices, and pushing them beyond their limits—in particular, the limits that have been imposed by our course curriculum and by the core-beliefs that mark the boundaries between student and scholar. In order to accomplish all of this work, I use three strategies: 1. I ask self writing students to read demanding and difficult texts; 2. I ask them to practice an intensified reading-writing relationship; and 3. I ask them debate with me (to affirm and to challenge) the concepts and claims rendered in the texts they read and produce.

As such, I have upper-level essay students read difficult, contemplative, even polemical works—works that are generally reserved for the experts, for scholars. Notably, these are works that are not chosen according to their canonical value or according to whether they will turn up on the GRE. Too, I don't have them move through those texts in a single day or in a week, like we do in our literary theory course or in our upper-level rhetoric and writing course. Instead, we take such texts at about ten pages per class period—and sometimes (especially when we are reading Nietzsche) much less, e.g., 2-3 pages per class period. We also return to those texts repeatedly, throughout the course of the semester. In short, I don't worry about how much they are reading in these courses; I worry about *how* they are reading. In reading such texts at a much slower pace, students learn to read like scholars, to take their time with the texts, to struggle through them, to focus (like scholars do) on a single word or phrase for as long as it takes for them to make that word/phrase do some work for them.

I want for my students to mimic the deliberate and attentive reading practices of scholars, but in order to explain what deliberateness and attentiveness look like, I point to imitation practices in the ancient world. Of reading, Quintilian states, "For a long time, too, none but the best authors must be read, and such as are least likely to mislead him who trust them; but they must be read with attention, and indeed with almost as much care as if we were transcribing them [...]" (129; book X, ch. 1, sec. 20).[37] The key to Quintilian's call lies in his assertion that we read "as if we were actually transcribing what we read." The practice of reading works in tandem with writing-in-response to those readings.

By building on any effort to transcribe the work of another (the "already said") into their own writings and within the context of their own questions, students will find themselves essaying in the meditative ways I've described in Chapter 4. The essays they produce, then, will not be the navel-gazing essays we are used to seeing in creative nonfiction courses. Instead of "pursu[ing] the unspeakable," "reveal[ing] the hidden," or "say[ing] the unsaid," as Foucault characterizes the work of confessionary writing (like the contemporary personal essay), the self writing essay is an attempt at "captur[ing] the already said," "collect[ing] what one has managed to hear of read, and for a purpose that is nothing less than the shaping of the self" ("Self-Writing" 211).[38]

To help students into this very different relationship with texts, I require my students to keep an Annotation Notebook, which is a variation of the *hupom-*

nēmata, meant to enable a reading-writing connection, which in turn enables the "shaping of the self." This practice serves as the foundation for the work they will do throughout the semester. I begin my self writing course with Longinus's *On the Sublime*, and after the first class discussion of the first ten pages of the text, I assign the Annotation Notebook. Here is a copy of the Annotation Notebook Assignment:

> Directions: Please annotate the readings due for each class period in your Annotation Notebooks, following the guidelines below. Tasks numbered 1-3 can be addressed in any order you wish.
>
> 1. List key concepts, and as best you can, define them.
> 2. Explain, in your own words, the major question that the writer is exploring.
> 3. List key claims regarding that question (e.g., claims that answer, frame/contextualize, or complicate the question).
> 4. Note any insights in the text that you find to be interesting (e.g., insights that are compelling, curious, infuriating) in the following way: first, copy the passage in which you encountered the insight; then, reflect on the insight in one of two ways—by simply jotting a quick "note to self" about why it's interesting, or by freewriting in response to the passage. I should see at least one freewrite to one insight in each notebook entry.

In class, we use tasks 1-3 to guide the first half of the class period's discussion. In the first week or two, I stick to that guide closely. Only when I am sure that the students are grasping the key concepts, major question(s), etc., in each of the texts, will I move away from this format and begin class, instead, by unpacking a few of the denser or more problematic passages that I've selected. In addition, for the first couple of weeks with any text, we shift in the last half of class to task number four in their notebooks, and it is here that I see most clearly the creation of a relationship of oneself to oneself in my students' work.

For example, in Chapter 3 of *On the Sublime*, Longinus argues that false sentiment is one kind of writing defect that "militate[s] against sublimity." He states, "[false sentiment] is hollow emotionalism where emotion is not called for, or immoderate passion where restraint is what is needed. For writers are often carried away, as though by drunkennesss, in outbursts of emotion which are not relevant to the matter in hand, but are wholly personal, and hence tedious" (103). A few semesters ago, a student in one of my self writing courses wrote about this insight repeatedly in her Annotation Notebook, returning to it again and again, even as we moved to other texts that were investigating different concerns. In her final essay for the course, Longinus's insight served as material for an extended meditation in which she arrived at a new insight about her own artistic work. Specifically, this student turned her attention to her experiences with a painting she had created in the past and had shown in a local coffee shop, a painting that had frustrated her so much that she eventually took it back from the shop and stashed it under her bed, where it still sat, because she found that though she had created it in a fit of despair, it was consistently read by audiences as a symbol of hope. In her extended meditation, she eventually found that she had failed to convey the proper emotion because of the wholly personal and immoderately passionate conveyance of emotion and that her audience's inability to read the proper emotion in it felt like a betrayal, not only by that audience but by the art and by her self, as an artist.

I read this extended meditation as an example of one writer working in relation to her self on the page, through the truth test and the unification practices of self writing. Basically, she tested and integrated the "truth" forwarded by Longinus in regards to her own work, negotiating conceptions of her self-as-artist and her self-as-feeling, among others. Though she was working through a question ("why did the piece fail?"), the meditation served not only as a practice through which she could think-on-the-page, but it also served as a practice in which that self-on-the-page spoke back to her, as insight gave way to insight and relation to relation, until she came away from the exercise with a different sense of her self—as artist, as writer, as feeling-person.

I should note that I only discuss the "self-to-self" relation with my students in conceptual terms before they begin to draft their essays. I find that the concept is a tangle for them and only seems to confuse their writing processes, until they have generated an extended meditation which they, then, can engage and revise. At that point, they are able to recall and to experience the self-to-self relation that Foucault describes. Too, they are able to reflect on it in their journals (in which I ask them to freewrite each day at the end of class). In the end, many of my students have commented that it felt as though they met another self in writing—a self that may have been, in turns, fearful and tentative, thoughtful and capable. They often tell me that they believe they became stronger writers for it. I have always found that I have had to agree them.

I firmly believe that much of that strength comes, too, from my working to push these students beyond the limits I mentioned earlier and from them working so hard to reach beyond those limits. As I've explained, I push them, in part, by asking them to engage with difficult texts, like Longinus's *On the Sublime*. Admittedly, over the years, I've had colleagues advise me not to teach the philosophers, scholars, and essayists I love because, according to my colleagues, the teaching will spoil that love in failing to transfer to my students. I think I have felt that frustration before, though only with particular students who, in my most arrogant and dangerous moments, I believed could be helped or healed by reading a particular text. For the most part, I don't experience that "spoiling," though, and I suspect that this is because I include the Annotation Notebook and considerable (tough and demanding) debate in self writing courses. I'd love to sit in coffee shops and bars and debate with my peers the tenets of Nietzsche's and Levinas's and Derrida's work, like I did as a graduate student, but now, as I see it, my job is to carry that work into the classroom. This is what my graduate school professors did for me; I do it, now, for my students, graduate and undergraduate, alike.

Again, debate looks very different in a lower-level writing course than it does in an upper-level essay course, but my point here is to say that we don't have to be afraid for ourselves or for our students in bringing difficult and even our most-loved texts into the course; in fact, I think we limit our students' development, as thinkers and writers, when we deprive them of such experiences. My upper-level essay students are, quite simply, exhilarating (and often exhilarated) in their engagement with difficult texts, and I'll note that I don't teach at an ivy league or Research 1 university. My very positive experience is, in part, due to the fact that my colleagues do an excellent job training our students to read closely and thoughtfully (one of the great benefits of working in an English department). As one of only two Rhetoric and Composition Ph.D.s in our department, it then falls to me to teach our students to write beyond formulas. By the time I see them in an upper-level essay course, they are, I find, well trained, but perhaps too well trained—they are good at reading closely, good at writing in formulas, and they have come to accept that they cannot do anything else as good English majors and/or writing minors.

I believe—and I will provide evidence in this chapter of the fact—that students are fully capable of working productively with texts that continue to confound and frustrate, as well as entice and inspire, the very best scholars writing in the Humanities today. I dwell on this point at length here because I have found that it is only through this level of intensity in engaging with texts that students can practice self writing. In working with a group of upper-level essay students who know the value of exploration and who are beginning to believe that they, too, can interpret the work and make it do some work for them, the dense text begins to open itself. If they haven't already experienced it, self writing students come to know the depth of that experience: how our engagement with a text can reshape us; how that engagement is a process of frustration and pleasure, of confusion and realization; how that engagement draws us together, as a class, and how it becomes deeply personal and private, even as we are working together; how that engagement makes us feel stupid and brilliant in turns; and how, in the end, working with such texts is like learning to build a boat with what sometimes feels like a plethora of nails and no hammer—until we've figured out how to make a hammer from the exercise itself.

Some of the texts I've used in these courses have been Longinus's *On the Sublime*, Nietzsche's "Truth and Lies in a Nonmoral Sense," his *Genealogy of Morals*, *The Gay Science*, *Thus Spoke Zarathustra*, and *Ecce Homo*. I've used Richard Miller's *Writing at the End of the World* and Laura Kipnis's *Against Love*. In the next self writing course I teach, I will incorporate works by Kenneth Burke. I use texts that confound me, but that I've also found to be revelations in each reading. With each of these texts, I find myself saying to my students, "Here's something about which I have no idea what to think. What do you think of it?" It is in such moments, too, that I often reach back into my writing training to a perhaps surprising exercise—the freewrite.

I typically ask students to freewrite when I anticipate that they will have strong feelings/beliefs about an issue—e.g., when Nietzsche claims that God is dead in *The Gay Science*. I ask for them to freewrite when I have a question I can't yet begin to formulate for them for discussion—e.g., something about Miller's insight into how we internalize socially sanctioned moralities and how Kipnis's polemic fails to undo that internalization, because of something about the internalization process, itself. Or, I ask them to freewrite when I feel like we've gotten too far away from their essays and I want them to have a chance to trace connections. As a rule, I don't grade freewrites. I tell students that if they'd like me to see the freewrites, then they may turn them in; however, the freewrites are only intended to help students to consider claims, to test ideas, to draw connections. Too, as I mentioned above, in the freewrite, they have the opportunity to address and acknowledge their initial emotional responses to what are often polemical statements, which I believe is essential to their success in the course. If they have a strong emotional response, there must be a safe space for them to articulate it—and to work their way through it.

I have found that the freewrite is so useful to the self writing course that I require all of us, including myself, to keep Freewriting Journals and to write in them at least once during each class meeting. As such, this is another way, like the use of debate, in which the work of the course becomes a more collaborative effort; the students see me working along with them to explore ideas and sort out feelings. That's not to say that I'm not the teacher; I am both teacher and mentor in such a course. However, this (collaborative effort) is just as important as the use of challenging readings in the self writing course: students must be encouraged to take ownership of the work of the course. The Freewriting Journal, when one is maintained by each class member (including the teacher), can assist in that goal. In short, in seeing me do what I'm asking them to do, students will not only understand but are more likely to be convinced of the value of the work—e.g., that freewriting *is*, actually, a scholarly practice; that it is as useful to me as I tell them it should be to them.

To sum up, then, these are the common assignments (and practices) in my self writing courses that I've discussed so far:
- Demanding readings, treated in short sections
- The Annotation Notebook
- The Freewriting Journal
- Class Discussion—which really works more like debate in that students are invited to affirm and to challenge claims and concepts (made in a text, by peers, or by me)

This list leaves just two more essential assignments for any self writing course:
- Formal essays
- Workshops of peer essays

MEDITATION AS ESSAYING (AND VICE VERSA)

Of course, the essay, itself, should be a practice of meditation, of self writing, as has been shown in Chapter 3. However, I find that I can't simply offer students an essay assignment that asks them to participate in all of the practices of self writing right away. I have to do some work around the concept of subjectivity in the essay with them first. To do so and, simultaneously, to create a bridge between the reading and writing practices that I've explained above and the self writing practices I'll eventually ask them to participate in for their essays, I have, in the past, offered an essay assignment that centers in the practice of imitation. This assignment enables students' reflection on the practice of imitation within the particular conceptions of subjectivity I've presented in Chapters 1-3. Here's an example of such an essay assignment:

> For this essay assignment, you will try your hand at the kind of exercise many of your essay-parents practice(d)—imitation. I will give you a copy of one of Samuel Johnson's essays from *The Rambler*. Johnson is perhaps the most famous essayist of the 18th Century. I thought of Johnson's work because of your writings and our ongoing discussions of writing practices and

voice [I use Johnson's essay No. 2. Saturday, 24 March 1750].

I'd like you to imitate the section assigned to you. Make his expression your expression. This means you'll have to figure out what, exactly, he is doing in essaying. What concept/belief/issue is he expressing or exploring? How is he doing so? Stick closely to what you think he's doing. For example, if he explores a topic, by using a personal anecdote, you do the same by using a personal anecdote. If he criticizes a political belief, you do so.

You don't have to change every word in every section to make the expression yours. For example, in the first sentence of the essay, Johnson is talking about the mind. You, too, can use the word "mind," but you will have to find your own way of arguing, "That the mind of man is never satisfied…." (if arguing is what you think he's doing, of course).

Imitation is a difficult exercise, sometimes tedious, sometimes overwhelming. This is one essay assignment that students most consistently suffer over. So, start early, and talk to me if you have any questions or concerns.

My students always (and often, passionately) agree that the exercise is difficult. They find that they've had to read and reread the essay many times, to look up lots of words, and to draft over and over again their imitative essays. This exercise is, of course, an act of meditation, and in it, they are not only trying to grasp the content of Johnson's essay but are also trying to rewrite it so that the imitation does what the original does and the way that the original does it—which means that they have to figure out not only what the essay's content is but how it works (e.g., via inquiry or argument or skepticism or confession).

Inevitably, given the essay's relationship to the essayist, the question of what constitutes the self comes to the forefront of the work. Students who believe that the self-on-the-page, i.e., the voice, is a reflection of their essential self will often state that the assignment is unfair or even impossible because Johnson's essay must be an expression of who he is; therefore, any imitation, consequently, is going to fail at doing what he did. Too, the student cannot express his/her true self, if s/he is confined to doing so by writing about and in the same ways as another writer. If, on the other hand, the student believes that his/her self-on-the-page is a social construct, then students tend to argue that the exercise is something like acting, where s/he tries to appropriate the truths and writing practices in Johnson's work and render them via the student's particular social persona—twisting them according to the writer's own gender, class, race, etc. In this framework, the question for the writer might become, "How does a white, middle-class female define 'the mind'?" However, in this conception of the self-on-the-page, my students always conclude that reconstructing social categories works too much like stereotyping and, thus, seems overly simplistic and dangerous. If one were to take seriously Foucault's version of subjectivity, though, then the exercise would be totally different—a kind of "thought experiment" and one in which the writer might participate in his/her own "shaping" via his/her work with the text.

What I love about this exercise is that no matter what conception of self the writer is invested in, the exercise works as a practice of meditation—because of the reading and writing required just to arrive at a decision about the conception of self that will inform the student's work. As one who is invested in the third version of subjectivity because of its productiveness in enabling debate, in enabling engagement and, even, change, I also like this exercise because it makes very clear to student essayists that the essay, when it is freed of the confines of the essential or socially constructed self, can be intensely generative, even when it is written via the practice of imitation. They see that, for example, when Johnson speaks of men's minds never being satisfied, the student essayist could create an imitative essay by testing this "truth," using some of the tactics Johnson does (e.g., through the use of example or inversion). But, the imitation would be meditative. The student could write, using the strategies Johnson does and covering the topics Johnson does, in order to test his methods and his claims—even his questions and the gaps in his work.

In preparation for this assignment, I would recommend studying these three versions of subjectivity and their implications with students. I usually use the above assignment later in the course, and as such, I emphasize in any conversation about the essay assignment the various conceptions of subjectivity and how they might determine the work each student does. That way, students can decide which conception of subjectivity they will be working within in imitating the text. This conversation (or more realistically, series of conversations) also helps to open up in compelling ways the next step in the process—workshopping the essays.

One of the first questions I ask of the student essayists who are invested in the concept of the essential self is how a reader can determine whether the text is an accurate expression of the writer. As many writing teachers and scholars have noted, it's clear that the reader can't, so the question becomes: what is the reader's role, then? How is that role helpful, and how is it limiting? I push them, too, to think about the reader as one who is not only an assessor or critic, but one who is reading for many other reasons (e.g., pleasure, competition, etc.). This expansion of the student's conception of the reader also invites the question of what one gets from reading someone else's essential self.

The second option—that the text is the socially constructed self of the writer—is equally complex and has just as many (and profound) proliferative effects, for as my students quickly point out, they are very often not able to tell from the text the writer's race, social class, ethnicity, sexual orientation, or his/her gender. They find that, as readers, they are imposing these categories on the text, based on what they know of the flesh-and-blood writer whose name is attached to the piece—a practice few seem comfortable with, when they become aware of it. Too, the question of what one can get from an essay that is the construction of another writer's self comes up: such an essay can offer individuals, particularly those of marginalized groups, a vision of a self that may not be available to them in mainstream media and in academic discourse; however, as I've argued in Chapter 2, that vision is of a category—or a series of categories—of self, which is limiting (and potentially dangerous in that limiting).

In the third option, if readers critique the student essay based on how well it engages with the truths forwarded and the practices at work in Johnson's essays, then they are practicing a different kind of critique. Granted, students tend to flounder in figuring out what the practices are in Johnson's essay, but this is where I put them together in groups and let them figure it out together. After reading the essay on their own, working through it with peers, and thinking through the subjectivity question, they are so familiar with Johnson's essay that they are able to move rather quickly through their peers' essays to identify any imitation of Johnson's practices in each. For example, they can easily identify the use of quotes, the explicit references to the reader, and the subsequent challenges to claims made earlier in the essay.

In the end, they have the opportunity to explore—even at the personal level—the various conceptions of subjectivity and what each means for the writer's relationship to the page, to its content, to the writing practices the student participated in while making that page, and to any critique of his/her work (as well as to his/her critique of others' work). As one might easily imagine, the exploration of all of these relationships in which the writer works and is constituted also gives students the opportunity to explore the complexities of other relations: e.g., writer-text-reader-context relations. Meaning is complicated in all of those relations and in ways that are so pronounced that students begin to see just how mutable meaning is, as well as what might be at work to make one meaning more customary than others.

In a similar way, I like to give students the same text to read at different times over the course of the semester so that they can see how the meanings (and even the strategies) of the text mutate according to what we've read, what we've talked about and written about, what is going on in their lives, etc. For example, one of the first assignments that I give in my essay classes is to ask students to read Nietzsche's "Truth and Lies in the Nonmoral Sense." Then, at the end of course, they return to the same essay and read it again. Their experience with it changes with each reading. I would argue, in fact, that their experience with it expands with each reading because the meditation intensifies. This practice becomes especially important when pushing students beyond imitation exercises like the one I included above into what, I think, are more sophisticated meditative exercises.

For example, here's another essay assignment which asks for students to imitate the mode of engagement in other works. This kind of assignment, I use not primarily to test the implications of writers' buy-in to particular conceptions of subjectivity but in order to further help them into the practices of self writing. Through it, I try to push them out of their "comfort zones" and encourage them to try out some of the practices ("the methods," as I refer to them in the assignment) that other creative nonfiction writers use. In such ways, I'm asking them to practice self writing (practicing the disparate and unification, for example) without bogging them down in Foucault's terminology. Here's a sample assignment:

> Your second essay for this course should explore a particular topic/question, using at least one of the methods of exploration we've seen used in the texts we've read so far in class and responding to a series of outside sources that also engage, on some level, with your topic. You might use Plato's dialectical method; you might practice relentless skepticism, like Nietzsche; you might create a fragmented text and position the fragments in ways that cultivate connections and raise questions among seemingly disparate parts, like Miller. Depending on what method of exploration you use, the incorporation of those outside sources should work within that method. For example, if you are practicing skepticism in the essay, then even if you initially use one source to critique another, you'll eventually be critiquing ideas presented in all of your chosen sources.

You'll notice that I introduce this as the second essay assignment students write for this particular self writing course; the first essay assignment in the course asks them to engage at length with, by examining multiple perspectives on, a topic that comes out of the class readings and/or discussion. In the first assignment, I'm essentially asking them to experiment with the truth test, which I first explained in Chapter 3. I offer these assignments in this order so that students can, if they so choose, revise the first essay by, essentially, breaking its backbone and reworking it through a different series of practices that, consequently, create a different essay.

The first time I offered this assignment, I was impressed with the work the students produced. I'm including here a sample essay, produced by one such student. To my knowledge, he had little training in creative nonfiction/the personal essay when he walked into the course. He was a quiet and thoughtful student: he rarely talked in class, but he was always there, scribbling in his Freewriting Journal. Here's the essay he wrote in response to the prompt above:

Cameron Markway
4530 words

Understanding We

The darkness isn't as bad as I once thought. My eyes can adjust to anything. The light only distracts from the actual knowing of an object. After all, isn't vision a liar, making me see what I wish, altering my interpretations of events? Do I actually *see* what is in front of me? And what about you? Are you able to see the light, or are you "overwhelmed by the sun's beams?" (Plato 65). Perhaps darkness is more of a friend than we believe, or perhaps not. The choice is not up to us anymore, is it?

Before birth. This is when it doesn't matter; this is when it matters most. This is when understanding of who we are is already packed into the yet-to-be-born vessel of ourselves. It is that darkness that we identify with, living forever around us and inside of us. We don't remember it; we can't comprehend it, but it is at this time that we are the most complete. We recognize every aspect of ourselves without even consciously recognizing it. We *are* every part of ourselves. There is no need to consciously recognize the good and the bad within us before our delivery into the realm outside of the womb. It is the introduction to the light that triggers the loss. We are no longer part of ourselves, no longer known only to ourselves.

Self Writing in the Classroom

Upon our introduction into the world, we become part of everyone else. We are for our family. We are for our friends. We are for all others. We have lost what it means to be our *self*.

The feeling presents itself in the form of a headache, a dull throbbing that is never quite painful but never quite pleasant. It spawns recognition within me of my lack of understanding. One of those unexplainable feelings of doubt and unworthiness that all of those emo bands tend to sing about, presented in the form of a question that has been contemplated by stoners probably from the first time marijuana was used as a drug: Who am I, man?

The question carries more baggage than the new Boeing 787 Dreamliner, baggage that keeps regenerating every time one piece is removed. Not even the most adept baggage handler would be able to unload a cargo hold containing this large of a load. I, being the feeblest of all these metaphorical workmen, will not fool myself into thinking that I will be able unload even the smallest portion of this luggage, but at least I can try to unload a couple bags and deliver them to a location that might fit. After all, even if I do send an item to the "wrong" location, that item can either be repacked and sent back or made to work for whomever it was sent to. There is no correct destination for the luggage in this mentally constructed airport; it can get tossed around and delivered a thousand times to the same location without a single complaint, or it can be delivered once and disappear.

Nothing is for certain; nothing is not for certain. We are an enigma to ourselves, more clearly and more falsely seen through the eyes of others than through our own eyes. We just keep refilling with the thoughts of others, the thoughts of our own creation (if that is possible). We just keep getting tossed around in the cargo hold of our minds, never really discovering, never really finding the correct destination for this thought or that thought. We just keep being ourselves without knowing what ourselves are.

It was easier for me as a child. My identity was my name and a list of what I liked and what I did not like.

-Hi, my name is Cameron.

-Hello, Cameron.

-I like football, hunting, candy, and cartoons.

-Thank you, Cameron. You may take your seat.

What a fantastic way to view the world. This was me. I was football. I was hunting. I was candy. And I was cartoons. I was Cameron. Period. It was never complicated. My parents would hang my pictures of fish on the refrigerator with tape. This is how I knew I was awesome. Tape was never fun to take off of a refrigerator. My pictures deserved the extra effort. This is how I understood the world around me: This gets me recognition, so I will keep doing this in order to get recognition.

-I got an A on my book report, Mom.

-Good job, son. Here is a piece of candy.

-Thanks.

-Now run along and play.

My identity took shape. I had become a product of the reward-punishment system. I was like Pavlov's dog, conditioned to drool at the thought of a picture on the refrigerator or a piece of candy in my hand. I was controllable. I was malleable. I was constructed. And I was a child. I was Cameron. Period.

There is some part of humans that helps them to accept their positions. Some people are content to live in the position they were placed in to begin with. They accept their places like they are living in some sort of universal caste system, unable to escape the limits that society has placed on them. They live as part of the majority, losing themselves in the crowd. To escape this system, there has to be a realization that develops from within, a realization that one must not live for the majority for the betterment of the majority but must live for oneself for the betterment of the whole. "One's group identity is always a mask" (Steele, "White Guilt"). Without this realization, we will all become one; we will all be wearing the same mask.

I was in middle school. I had taken on a new understanding of myself since those days of refrigerator pictures and candy-coated rewards. Yesterday's excitement had become today's childish delights—something to be avoided if one was ever to drink the sweet nectar of the popular kids. My identity had become whatever the identity of the "in group" wanted it to be. "I am whatever you say I am" (Eminem, 'The Way I Am"). I was listening to the music everyone else was listening to, playing sports with the popular kids, rebelling against the math teacher just because everyone hated math (even though, at the time, I was good at it).

-Do you like the math teacher?

-He isn't bad. I don't mind him.

-Well, I hate that guy. Math sucks.

-You're right. I don't really like him either. Math does suck.

At the time, it didn't feel like I was losing myself; I just wanted to be popular. And being that I was an overweight kid in a hostile middle school environment intensified my yearning for popularity. Life wasn't about carving out my own niche; life was about being the same, being like everyone else. I was me. My friends were me. My sports were me. My school was me. I was so focused on everyone else's approval that everyone else became what I wanted to be. The majority never looked so unique. I wanted, as an individual, to see myself reflected in the masses, to look in the mirror while standing next to a friend and be unable to distinguish one from the other. This was my dream: to be a blank puzzle piece in the box of one thousand other blank pieces. I wanted nobody to question me on what I liked or what I wanted because I wanted what I liked and what I wanted to be the same as what everyone else liked and wanted. Hiding *my* interests and not bringing them out in public became the way to remain "safe." I was normal. I was popular. I was Cameron. And I was everyone. I was wearing the same mask as everyone else.

"Where someone rules, there are masses; and where we find masses we also find a need to be enslaved" (Nietzsche 195).

The danger of living for the majority, of relating to the majority so easily, is that we stray farther from ourselves than is healthy. We start to lose sight of who we are, and in doing so, we start to form an identity not of our own unique structure but of a structure dictated by the masses. We walk away from ourselves, no closer to knowing who we are than when we were first released into the world. The worst part of this group identification comes with being content to live with the identity that has been bestowed upon us by others. Contentment is the most dangerous feeling, and it is also the easiest to fall into. With contentment comes the inability to question, and without the ability to question we will never be able to know our *self*.

There is a time when everyone has to grow up. Isn't that what our elders always told us? Attached to that advice were other generic pieces of what, at one time, sounded like profound wisdom: You can't please everyone. Be yourself. Don't do it just because your friends are doing it (If all of your friends jumped off of a bridge, would you?).

    -You can't please everyone, Cameron.

    -Wow, you are absolutely right. That is where I have been going wrong this whole time. Thanks, <u>Insert ANY name here.</u>

    -I'm glad I could help.

    -You are the best.

This is what I call, in this new technologically advanced era, "Facebook advice." But I used to think this type of advice came straight from the heart. At least, it did always make me feel better about my situation. I was becoming content with the lifestyle I was living, getting by with the advice I was given. I was slipping into the murky waters of "fineness." Everything will take care of itself. I wasn't doing any real growing up; I was only following the advice of others. I was attempting to expand myself, to understand myself without the knowledge of how to go about understanding myself. It was a premature attempt at growth that only tightened the mask on my face, forcing me deeper and deeper into the group identity, making me lose myself at a more rapid rate than ever before.

Maybe it is not until we sink to our lowest point that we can finally look up and see the stars. We have been forever spiraling down, being twisted and distorted for so long that we were never able to get a clear view of what was around us. The bottom provides some stability; it provides a painful realization that we are no longer ourselves. The mask we have been wearing for so long, the group identity that has created us and shaped our lives, is beginning to crack. Darkness seeps through the fissure, reminding us of the time when we were part of ourselves, living inside the womb, before we were exposed to the light that so rudely blinded us and turned us

Chapter Five

away from ourselves. The bottom provides a much needed awakening. Here is where we begin to realize that something is wrong, allowing us to open our eyes and embrace the darkness that surrounds us. We don't see a thing, but we experience the comfort that the darkness provides. But only for a short time. We must reenter the light, while attempting to remember the darkness. We will be blinded at first, but the memory of the darkness will keep us pushing forward.

The early college years. I was still living with the mask of the group identity upon my face, but it was beginning to itch. There was something wrong with the way I was living. All those years of living for the group, whether it was family or friends, whether it was willingly or, to an extent, unwillingly, had to come to an end. I was lost at the bottom of my 19-year hole. It had taken me this long to realize that I had lost myself somewhere along the way. But a change was coming, a change I could feel within myself. Before I realized this problem inside of me, I was drinking all of the time, getting high before classes, ditching school to party, but it stopped feeling right.

I began to recognize all the negative parts of myself, parts that I didn't even realize were negative until this self-reflection. I realized that I had not been living *for* me; I had been living *as* those around me lived. I was a part of something on the outside, something bigger; it dictated the choices I made, the people I hung out with, the movements of my thoughts. I was calling myself into question, using one side of my brain to interrogate the other.

-What is your problem? Why have you made these choices?

-You are part of me. You should know the answer.

-Why are I here, you?

-You know us to be parts of one both.

The language got scrambled. Two sides of a whole pitted against one another. The throbbing increased in my head. No coherent answer presented itself as to why or how I wanted to make a change. The negatives all got mixed into one until that final eruption, the volcano of my mind, the sudden burst of molten light that rose high into the air and then coated the world with the dark layer of ash, coated *my world*. I could breathe again in the darkness. The ash filled my lungs, and I could breathe out dust, a yet-to-be-formed idea that needed time to solidify. It was only a question.

I just wanted to fit in? The statement had morphed, had altered its appearance and turned into a question. Did I want to fit in? Did I want to be part of something, part of the group identity? No, not any longer. I wanted to be part of myself. I wanted to realize my full potential without realizing what my full potential was. I wanted to take a step in a direction that would set me apart from the group. I was awake inside my own head, making changes for myself that I would never have dreamed about in the past. I changed my major, stopped partying so much, distanced myself from the majority. This is when the dull throbbing began; this is when it got painful and scary. I had finally broken away from the group identity, but I still didn't have an identity of my own. I was finding my *self*, yes, but I was nowhere near complete. My mask had become blank, but I was still wearing a mask.

Knowing that there is a piece missing on the inside is only the beginning of understanding who we are. The mask that we wore for so long, the mask of the group identity does not just fall off when we realize we are not truly our own *self*. The mask might remain in place forever, changing shape as our experiences grow with our own personal interests and understandings. Will it ever go away?

Chapter Five

Maybe it is a futile endeavor, this trying to know thyself. If it takes a lifetime to accomplish with no actual guarantee of accomplishment, then what is the point? I can just as easily live happily wearing any mask. After all, are humans not social beings, designed to mingle and reproduce and prosper—together? I want my friends. I want my family. I want my girlfriend and my classmates and my professors. I live in happy ignorance of myself when I feel it is necessary to do so. I become part of the group, part of the student body that makes up the twelve-thousand or so people who attend the University of Northern Colorado. I claim to want to know myself while at the same time claiming to be part of a bigger group of people. My dreams revolve around ideas of doing something great, something to change something else (Ahh, the hopes of the mind and the dreams of the youth). But, even if I were to realize my dreams, to become someone "unique," someone who changed the world, wouldn't I still be lumped into a group? There seems to be no escape, no possible way to shed the mask of the group identity without being forced to sport a new mask of a new group with a new label. It is a circle, perhaps.

Are we forever rotating? Do we join a group at one stage in our life, break from that group to discover our *self*, and then reposition ourselves within a different group until that group begins to lack what we need to progress? This seems to be the case. Without complete isolation from any group influence whatsoever, the idea of actually *knowing thyself* seems to be only a dream. With so much outside influence and so many ideas already floating around in the ocean that is the mind (and not just our own minds but the minds of other individuals, because, yes, we all share similar thoughts no matter whether or not we have met), is it even possible, with such a large number of people inhabiting the earth, to call oneself unique? Is it even possible that we can have a self of our own?

"Laws are necessary, of course, for no single individual, however good and co-operative, can have precise knowledge of the total needs of the community. Laws point the way to an emergent pattern of social perfection—they are guides. But, because of the fundamental thesis that the citizen's desire is to behave like a good social animal, not like a selfish beast of the waste wood, it is assumed that the laws will be obeyed" (Burgess 18).

Anthony Burgess may have been right. What happens if we use his fictional representation of the future as a model for the present, as a model for our mind. The laws would become our own thoughts, uncontrollable and all powerful, holding us back from breaking the rules of the majority because our thoughts know what is best for us. Our thoughts become our guides on the way to becoming perfect as a whole, a group of people sharing an identity. Is this the perfection we have been seeking out? Are we really programmed from the start "to behave like a good social animal"? After all, don't we sometimes want to blend with the crowd, go unnoticed in a cloud of faces, unrecognized and undisturbed. Do we not prize functioning members of society—members who contribute to the greater good of the community—over all others? These if-he-helps-me-I-will-help-him scenarios seem to be the standard operating procedure of society. Who would want to be known as "a selfish beast"?

I want to remove it, but it has ceased to be just a superficial covering over my face. I want to feel the flesh underneath, but the substance underneath is no longer what one would call or could call "flesh." I want to scratch the itch of understanding that is building under my mask, but there is no seam, no strap to simply remove, no button to push for automatic removal. It feels like a horror movie, this inability to remove the covering from my face. I struggle to find some sort of opening and am left with broken fingernails and blood on my hands. But the blood is not from my hands; it is from the mask. I look in the mirror and see the "face," unrecognizable and battered to a pulp. I crave that darkness that I used to know; I close my eyes. For too long has the mask been upon my face. Like a neglected house pet with a too-tight collar the mask has grown into my "flesh." It has ceased to be a real mask, ceased to be a mere covering up of who I really am; it has become part of me, part of my make-up, part of my everything. When I smile, I can feel the mask move with my facial muscles. When I touch my forehead, I can feel my fingers caressing what has now become part of me. I am a stranger to myself, but I am also new, somewhat reborn. I close my eyes even tighter. This is the darkness that I once knew. The darkness I understood before I knew I was able to understand. The mask has ceased to itch. Me, I have ceased to itch. This is my face. Maybe I have accepted my place. Maybe I have accepted that the mask that I so longed to remove was never really able to be removed. After all, what would I even look like without it? How would I be complete without it, after being through so much with it as my companion? This is how I understand myself, isn't it?

I'm in a classroom with some of my classmates for the first time ever. I know not a single person in the room.

   -Class, what do you think when you see this picture?

   -Praying mantis! (two students at once)

Two students, neither knowing anything about the other, say the same thing. Both have had different experiences in their lives, but they say the exact same thing. Although this example is very simple, it helps to explain why, perhaps, we cannot ever be our own *self*. Especially today, with all of the sharing of thoughts and ideas, the free social media sites where people can post thoughts (fully developed or otherwise), and the exchange of emails and the watching of television programs. Are any of our thoughts our own? It seems that we are just compiled of various words and phrases that have been said throughout time, repeated over and over in different generations by different people. Myself: I am built from the words of my parents, influenced by the thoughts of my friends, directed by the instruction of my teachers, but I am living in a body of my own. Who am I, man? I guess this is when it gets tricky.

Even now—sitting in my room by myself, surrounded by the air around me, writing my thoughts down in what I hope to be a coherent paper—am I only a part of myself? Is this alone time bringing me closer to realizing who I am? After all, this topic is of my choosing; my fingers are doing the typing; my brain is forming all of the sentences on the page. Right? But then I think about it. These thoughts in my head are not completely my own; these words I am writing have come before me; these ideas that I am incorporating in my paper have been altered by the feedback of my peers, by all of you who are reading this paper. All of you have contributed to this document in one way or another, have placed your thoughts within my head, have given me the comments and compliments that have altered my thinking. The question of "Who am I?" has become even more obscure. The more I try to develop my reasoning and sort out my thoughts, the more I find myself looking inside books to find quotes from people who think similarly or who have something smart to say that will help clarify what I am trying to explain. Is this what knowing thyself is? Can I only know myself through others' ideas and others' learning?

"There is a time in every man's education when he arrives at the conviction that envy is ignorance; that imitation is suicide; that he must take himself for better or for worse as his portion; that though the wide universe is full of good, no kernel of nourishing corn can come to him but through his toil bestowed on that plot of ground which is given to him to till" (Emerson 533).

Maybe this is the answer or, if not an answer, a beginning. Maybe *my* life story (my experiences, my friends, my good and bad decisions, my family) makes me *me*. Maybe knowing myself, knowing *thyself* is working with what has been given to me. Maybe the moving from group identity to group identity and wearing the masks of different groups at different times is what helped to produce the land on which I will begin to cultivate. After all, one cannot build one's experiences in a vacuum. I was *given* the land to till by others, and the others, to an extent, have a say in what I plant. After all, if the land is located in a mental environment that is cold, there will be no planting of bananas. I can only control how much I plant, can only choose from a limited variety of produce, but I at least have that control, and I guess that is all I can really ask for?

Who am I, man? I don't know yet. I know where I have been. I know what I like and dislike. I know the Denver Broncos are my favorite football team, and I love to read. I know that my family and friends have had such a huge impact on my life that I am thankful to have them as *part* of me, but not me. My *self*, that is where it gets tricky. I don't fully know. I think I am still like Emerson's farmer, planting and growing and harvesting and replanting. Maybe one year a crop will not grow, a harvest will not be completed, or a field will be neglected, but I will keep coming back. I will experiment with new crops, use new equipment to provide nutrients for my land, for my mind, for all of those who have helped to begin the process.

We define ourselves in different ways, never really finishing until we are dead, and even then—if we leave something or someone behind—we are still being defined in the minds of others. It's not so bad to not know who we are, because if we knew that we might not be willing to step out of our comfort zones. If we know our *self* too well, there is no room to change, and in an ever-changing world, that is suicide.

But today is when it comes full circle.
The Night collides with the Day;
a Serpent eating its tail begs for more
Inside the brain of an empty skull
bleached by Sun and darkened by
pain and terror. A gaze
from the sand-filled sockets creates
a shadowy vision of what is to come.
The Hidden Enemy waits behind, splitting its soul in two.
The mirror gazes back and looks inside itself.
The image smiling back is of itself.
But something more,
something better, and
something worse.
It has seen the other side of One.
The One whose other side is Nothing.
But today is when it comes full circle.
The Night collides with the Day;
Nothing makes sense.
But now it is all clear.

Works Cited

Burgess, Anthony. *The Wanting Seed*. New York: Norton, 1996. Print.

Emerson, Ralph Waldo. "Self-Reliance." *The Norton Anthology: American Literature*. Shorter 7th ed. Ed. Nina Baym. New York: Norton, 2008. 532-550. Print.

Eminem. "The Way I Am." *The Marshall Mathers LP*. Aftermath Entertainment/Interscope Records, 2000. CD.

Nietzsche, Friedrich. *The Gay Science*. New York: Vintage, 1974. Print.

Plato. "The Allegory of the Cave." *History Guide.org*. 13 May 2004. Web. 31 March 2012.

Steele, Shelby. "The Age of White Guilt: And the Disappearance of the Black Individual." *Harper's Magazine*. Nov. 2002. Web. 31 March 2012.

Works Consulted

Arnold, Matthew. "The Function of Criticism at the Present Time." *Critical Theory Since Plato*. Ed. Hazard Adams. New

Chapter Five

> York: Harcourt, Brace, Jovanovich, 1971. 592-603. Print.
> McLeod, Saul. "Ivan Pavlov." *Simply Psychology.org*. Simply Psychology, 2008. Web. 31 March 2012.
> McLeod, Saul. "Asch Experiment." *Simply Psychology.org*. Simply Psychology, 2008. Web. 1 April 2012.

I love Cameron's essay because it's doing so much imitative work, yet he's made it his own through the intense practices of meditation found in self writing. He begins with a question (which is a strategy I encourage in self writing assignments in order to help students into meditative practices). For Cameron, the question is, essentially, "who am I," but the question evolves in complex and compelling ways so that the essay is less about who he is and more about how [his] self is made. To explore this question, he structures the essay, at least on the surface, chronologically—starting with birth and moving through a few major life stages. However, upon further examination, it's clear to me that he is actually imitating Richard Miller's strategic use of fragmented text (in *Writing at the End of the World*)—positioning the fragments of text in such a way that the connections between sections (or the gaps) are opportunities for meaning-making, as much as (if not more than) a traditional transition might be.

For example, in the section that begins, "I was in middle school," Cameron uses at least two structures he's used in prior fragments: the dialogue between himself and a fictional other, as well as a particular syntactical sentence structure to designate a blurred subject-object relation (e.g., "My sports were me. My school was me"). Both structures call up, in this section, their uses in prior sections (e.g., in an earlier section, he said, "I was football. I was candy"). In that calling-up, the fragments of text are brought into explicit relation with one another—made to speak to each other, suggesting the development (through repetition and relation) of a particular idea among them.

For me, though, what is most interesting here is not necessarily the relation established between each fragment/section of text, but Cameron's use of a kind of mirroring sentence structure. That structure ("I am it. It is me.") is not one we discussed, as a class, when we talked about Miller's work. It is, to my mind, Cameron's attempt at taking the relation he's working to create among these fragments of text to another level—to the sentence level. In that syntactic relationship, he suggests the conceptual relationship that he will talk about explicitly later in the essay: the idea that his identity is structured according to "the masses" (including the masses' language, ways of making meaning, and ways of identifying the self). Cameron arrives at this realization, through the use of strategic pairing of fragments of text, like Miller does, but also through his use of the mirroring of sentence-structures. In short, he's imitated Miller's use of fragmented texts, but also intensified the imitation, making a new kind of pairing at the sentence level in his essay.

In addition to the ways in which Cameron has imitated and transformed Miller's particular use of strategic pairings, Cameron has, of course, essayed new content. In part, the content is "new" because of the structures. For example, looking at the same section (that begins with "I was in middle school"), Cameron arrives at this insight: "I was Cameron. And I was everyone. I was wearing the same mask as everyone else." Then, the section ends, and a new section begins with a quote from Nietzsche: "Where someone rules, there are masses; and where we find masses we also find a need to be enslaved." The positioning of the prior section against the quote raises the stakes and deepens the exploration. According to Cameron, the desire for safety, which motivates one to conform to the masses (to identify with things and experiences and groups that are part of "the masses"), is related to the need to be enslaved. That relation is a terrible realization for him—he realizes in it that the relation between safety and enslavement costs him his self, or knowledge of his self.

"New" content is also made, though, in Cameron's engagement with the ideas presented by the scholars he's read—in particular, Nietzsche. That engagement enables several other crises (realizations that are utterly disruptive) in the essay. The two that seem most disruptive are these: the moment in which Cameron realizes that humans might be "forever rotating" from self-discovery to self-erasure with a group, as well as the moment that his exploration becomes mired in the tension between wanting "to behave like a good social animal," not wanting to be known as "a selfish beast" (both are quotes Cameron pulls from Nietzsche's work), yet wanting desperately to get free of the confines, the impositions of groups, of language, and of "the mask." Here, I believe that his investigation into how the self is made comes to a head. He's been clinging onto the hope, the ideal, of a totally autonomous and essential self—one born fully whole and utterly perfect. At this moment, though, he considers, at last, another possibility—a possibility suggested in Nietzsche's work.

In the end, after at least a couple of pages of one crisis after another, Cameron practices "affirmation." In its simplest terms, affirmation is the practice of accepting some truth (however situational and tentative) for the purpose of testing it out or "taking it seriously," which I explain to my students as meaning that they must play that truth out—testing it out in a variety of contexts and finding out what it costs them and what it gets them in each. For Cameron, this affirmative practice happens around the "truth" that "Maybe knowing myself, knowing *thyself*, is working with what has been given to me" (emphasis in original). Clearly, that is exactly what he's done in this essay. And, it is exactly the kind of affirmative practice that functions as the engine to Nietzsche's work:

he makes claims as bold and daring as "God is dead" through the affirmative practice—by taking seriously the various and related truths that others (e.g., philosophers) have refused for centuries.

Cameron's essay is ambitious work, and like Seneca says, the essay "resemble[s] [that which 'has left a deep impress upon you'] as a child resembles his father, and not as a picture resembles its original" (281). In the end, I can see the traces of Nietzsche's work and Plato's and Miller's, but this is an entirely new essay. And, in it is revealed a different self.

Finally, I include below a sample essay produced in response to what I like to call my "capstone" essay assignment. In it, students are encouraged to start where they are. If they've had some experience with meditative or self writing practices in prior essays, then I push them to move beyond deliberately mimicking the strategies used by other writers and to concentrate, instead, on the major practices of self writing: practicing the disparate (including the truth test) and unification. In other words, I use imitation as a way into this larger practice of meditation or self writing; then, once they are familiar with that larger practice, I ask them to concentrate on the particular practices that constitute self writing. Often, I send them to Foucault's "Self Writing" so that they can see what those particular practices are and how they constitute the larger practice of self writing. I warn/advise them that the writing should feel like "getting into the ring" with a difficult, high-stakes topic.

I negotiate much of this "pushing" in one-on-one conferences with the student. Not all are ready for this step in an advanced personal essay course. I include here a sample essay produced by a student (one of two out of a course of 15 students) who was, obviously, ready for that step. Here's her essay:

Holly Stimson
5740 words

"The intuitive man [...] aims for the greatest possible freedom from pain [... and] reaps from his intuition a harvest of continually inflowing illumination, cheer, and redemption—in addition to obtaining a defense against misfortune. To be sure, he suffers more intensely, when he suffers; he even suffers more frequently, since he does not understand how to learn from experience and keeps falling over and over again into the same ditch. He is then just as irrational in sorrow as he is in happiness [...] and will not be consoled."

"How differently [the rational man] who learns from experience

and governs himself by concepts is affected by the same misfortunes! This man [...] seeks nothing but sincerity, truth, freedom from deception, and protection against ensnaring surprise attacks... he executes his masterpiece of deception in misfortune."

—Nietzsche, "On Truth and Lies in a Nonmoral Sense"

Creativity: The Rational Man Bled Dry

I typed "Creativity" in the title line and began to think about the act of creating, particularly. And the moment I did, I found I couldn't write any more.

Strange that this word, "creativity," would be the death (or at least temporary paralyzation) of my creative thought. After all, creativity is the capacity to form something, to produce some artifact or do some action from the imagination, to invent. Whether that creativity comes from the soul, the heart, the body, the brain, I don't know definitively. But I've always operated under the notion that creativity is dependent upon the brain, perhaps not solely, but in many ways. It is the channel through which external inspiration is run, and it is the brain that processes internal musings as well as governs the most basic building blocks that make creative products possible: the moving of a paintbrush, the solving of a calculus equation, the uttering of language.

This basic premise made me wonder if my personal failure to create was due to some sort of mind starvation. Ever since leaving the world of high school and entering college, I've fed my intellect with reviewing and learning of the greats in my first chosen field of study: philosophy. I studied Kant and his categorical imperative, hoping that whether in his correctness or incorrectness I could find some system of morality for myself and the world; I immersed myself in the Greek greats, Plato and Aristotle, pouring over the allegory of the cave as I sought the sun myself, and admiring the rhetoric of that great rhetorician who provided me with a vehicle for effectively expressing and persuading; I considered the social construction

Chapter Five

of Nietzsche in an attempt to construct myself, and I wonder what it means for God to be dead; I examine power in flux and wonder at what power I have at any given moment as I read Foucault. I devoured logical sequences of premises leading to irrefutable, mathematical results, syllogisms in which statements that could only be either true or false and which lead to conclusions that were sound or unsound.

For a time, this black and white world was tremendously satisfying. It was a realm in which I could look, examine, and exclaim, "right!" or "wrong!" and have the opportunity to be flawless and correct. Then the waves of ethics and epistemology came crashing down on my philosophical bubble, and the endless possibilities, the endless hours spend in a maze of inquiry, eventually became exhausting. I discovered that really determining which statements were actually true or false was more difficult than theoretically declaring things true or false within an inconsequential hypothetical syllogism, and I began to yearn to land somewhere rather than voyaging on the unending philosophical sea made by those who came before me. Philosophy helped me see part of the map, but it left something to be desired—some human element, a connection that theories couldn't achieve. I wanted an island of my own on which to rest, not the island of name-the-philosopher-by-whose-ideas-you-live-your-life.

So, I set sail. I declared English as my major and moved on to literature, a place where I was certain I could spend the majority of my time reading stories of interest, stories I liked, and that would in turn fuel my creativity and cause a flare of inspiration for stories of my own. But I discovered that to truly be taken seriously in literature, I had to learn how to cleverly combine a number of ideas that existed for decades and centuries. I had to spend a good deal of time indulging the ideas of my professor and, seemingly, my peers, rather than actually caring about every weapon being a phallic symbol and colors always representing the same things depending on the context. I had landed on my island, yes, but I was running on shifting sand. *Beowulf* made an impact the first time. I was delighted to partake in a seminal epic; I wanted to understand the literary greats before me; I was determined to invest time in understanding the literary discourses of which I was now a part. And after all this, when I was assigned *Beowulf* again, I was pleasantly surprised to gain new insights in the second reading. By the third time I was assigned it, I began to feel lazy when I skipped reading it. I learned a hundred different ways to look at a hundred different texts from a hundred different people, and instead of opening my mind to possibilities, I began to feel off-balance, as if I were carrying too many stories and potential interpretations, and if I didn't drop some of them, I would take a tumble myself. Juggling these things had left little room for me to even hazard a guess about my own opinions regarding these stories, much less left room to create stories myself.

I left my island (probably after reading somewhere that "no man is an island") and returned to more philosophical undertakings, but this time of a different nature: I sailed oceans of religion. Perhaps I'd grown tired of categorizing myself by differences and wanted to instead categorize myself by similarities and a shared community; but regardless of that, I wanted to find myself, my story, my beliefs, which would, in turn, spark my creativity for a lifetime, surely. But no, religion wasn't that place. This leg of my journey was less sailing and more a tossing about of a toy ship on hurricane seas. For it was wonderful, intellectual, *rational* to be well schooled in the principle tenants of the eastern religions, in Daoism and Hinduism and Buddhism and all sorts of -isms. Being well-versed in Biblical themes lent itself well to my increasingly frustrated literary escapades. Concepts about Judaism and Islam were terrifically helpful to the academic image, for what appears smarter than understanding and tolerating on an intellectual level those who are often subjected to prejudices under those less wise and educated? But all this head knowledge—again, my brain—was not enough. There was something that could not be accessed. For I was allowed to describe five religions and even comment on their irrationalities or benefits while still being considered an academic, but admitting the one to which I adhered decreased my ethos, ruined my unbiased

Chapter Five

perspectives. Admitting a moral conviction was tolerable, if sometimes awkward, in classroom discussions, but papers cannot and should not be written about a feeling or conviction because in academia, faith cannot be rationalized and made into something arguable and researchable.

By this time, I finally, perhaps belatedly, wondered if I was over-stimulating my intellect while neglecting another part of myself, so I began to drink in poetry—Yeats, Dickinson, Seely, Levine. And once more my intellect at work: brilliantly over-emphasize and overlook. I was captured by forms and I forced rhyme and I spent hours thinking about what way I wanted to write a poem rather than picking up a pencil. I posted a thousand conflicting quotes from the greats on how to write poetry, and I never acted on one of them. I memorized half a dozen stanzas and forgot them after recitation. And most of all, I could not find a place from which to write, the source to fuel poetry, and I felt less a poet than ever before because for others this part seemed to be what came so naturally. I couldn't access the wellspring of feeling after spending so much time learning to block the flow, and poetry, too, escaped me.

And all the while, my mind never stopped. Though I began with a love for creativity and the written word, I became merely a bank of others' academic thought. Words fell flat; creativity felt like a myth. For though I speak of creativity in the broadest terms, creativity also, in essence, revolves around the faculties of language: reading, writing, and other such linguistic discourses. I don't hold that language is the height of creative achievement; rather, it is simply the capacity in which I and every human creates, it is the common medium for everyone, and it is more dear to me than other forms of creativity because I cannot remove it from what it means to be human. Take away the artist's palette, and she will find some other vehicle for her art, but take away language, and I cannot speak into the void; I cannot communicate; identity and humanity come crashing down.

* * * * *

To be at a loss for words meant I was stuck. I looked, but I didn't find. "This man, who at other times seeks nothing but sincerity, truth, freedom from deception, and protection against ensnaring surprise attacks […]."

Class periods passed, pages of lecture notes were filled, I and dozens of my peers received shiny "A+" marks for contributing meaningful comments on texts I'd half-read, and still my brain felt like a wasteland. The engaging philosophical discussions that had once captured my whole head and heart, the hours full of poetry readings and writings that had dazzled my love of language and rhythm, the stories that had once filled me with promise and possibility like a balloon filled with helium—gone. I could recognize a fallacy in a logical syllogism, but I could not creatively think about these texts and make connections or come to conclusions; I could rattle off a dozen scholars I'd read on the vernacular tradition, but I could not create and verbalize sentences representing my own thoughts on my peer's argument; I could explain a villanelle and a Rogerian argument, but I could not create an original poem or an original thesis by which I could stand and say, "This is mine." Creativity and its college pseudo-disguise, critical thinking, were lost to me. And I couldn't remember why.

It was as if I was only becoming conscious after some sort of physical trauma to my head. I couldn't remember what exactly went wrong. After a long and delightful day of school that loaded my head with wonderful things, I sat down to begin an essay, and I entitled it "Creativity Part 2" because it was a continuation of a previous exploration on creativity.

And that's the last thing I remember. Maybe there was more in the process of losing creativity, maybe the moment leading up to the loss is all I chose to remember rather than trauma of the moment of loss, but I remember no more. "[This man] now executes his masterpiece of deception […]."

* * * * *

If this is beginning to sound as though I have disavowed all

Chapter Five

my intellectual predecessors in order to pretend I don't stand on the shoulders of those who come before me, that isn't true. I haven't the will or belief to front such a foolish and fallacious claim. I revere the greats of my academic disciplines, even if I don't believe or adhere to every claim made by them. No, the problem is not with my intellectual predecessors.

In fact, I don't know what the problem is. I simply woke up one day and realized that every paragraph I write mimics whatever I read before it. The lengthy, poetic, convoluted syntax of Emerson; the strange technicalities of cummings; or the rigid, measured tones of scholarship—I was no longer my own. And what concerned me wasn't mimicry (which is, I've read, the highest form of flattery, is it not?). When I had to reach, research, cross-reference, and double-check myself against a college career of accumulated knowledge before writing a simple sentence regarding Plato, I felt dried up even in the middle of the floodgates of information at my beck and call. And that's when I realized I didn't even know why I bothered to write when the world was already flooded with a thousand discourses with or without me. I didn't even know who I was, aside from college student, sponge.

Why do I seem to have hit my creative end? I hope it is only temporary, but even so, why has it occurred? I've experienced the proverbial "writer's block," and this is not it. I still have the capacity for creativity in language, for even now I pen a sentence that has (probably) never been written, thus demonstrating that creativity. What, then, is the problem? Have I some defect that should take me off the production line of scholars? Was I never supposed to question creativity—or even myself—because I was meant to be learning all the possible answers?

"He executes his masterpiece of deception in misfortune, as the other type of man executes his in times of happiness."

Have I somehow lost myself in the midst of so many other ideas? Ah, but this would assume that I have some essential self to lose. That I am the sum of my feelings, intuitions, instincts, and that I am quite possibly destined to something because I am me. I would say that's not how I *feel*, but that would only further the case for this essential self, a self that is based on feelings. I would say that my internal crisis seems based more on the fact that, without creative thought, I have become merely an intersection, a passing of discourses, a product of everything swirling around and through me. But even then, I can't settle upon that notion, regardless of my feelings, because my eyes ache with too many words written and my head throbs with the stress of my dilemma and my body is still intact.

I question why, and though I may not show or admit it, I'm secretly afraid. "He wears no quivering and changeable human face, but, as it were, a mask with dignified, symmetrical features."

What is it that causes this desert state when, judging by my blossoming peers and by the commendation for the university experience, I should in fact be an oasis of intellectual ideas, critical thinking, and creativity? It isn't as though I have been robbed of all opinions by the overwhelmingly "better" opinions of others, for time and again I have shouldered a heavy and solid thesis and built an ironclad argument to support it. It isn't as though others' opinions have drowned mine out, leaving me incapable of generating opinions or expressing them, for I've started a dozen papers just today, each with different topics, quotes, and ideas. Yet, not one of them has grown to fruition; few made it past the first paragraph or two before hitting an invisible wall of which I cannot derive the origination.

* * * * *

How could this invisible wall exist in a world of constant learning? How could my creativity run dry when I drink constantly of the streams of the greatest creative minds on the planet? I cannot explain why, of course, because I have no creativity with which to generate such an answer. I could write the wonder whys, but the capacity to put more than one

Chapter Five

and one together eludes me, and that alarms me.

"He does not cry; he does not even alter his voice."

So, the ringing bell, the realization that I cannot realize because the realization has already passed. The intuitive man is dead. In its place, the rational man: "When a real storm cloud thunders above him, he wraps himself in his cloak, and with slow steps he walks from beneath it" (Nietzsche 1179).

The ultimate pay-off: that misfortune, the death of my own creativity, should turn out to be merely a bothersome storm cloud from which I can easily, calmly, rationally escape. Perhaps, if I rationalize further, this creativity is not even dead at all, but is rather a new incarnation of creativity that, instead of existing only with the intention "to express an exalted happiness," instead of "reap[ing] from [my] intuition a harvest of continually inflowing illumination, cheer and redemption," I have learned to steadily, rationally remove myself from misfortunes. Perhaps there is creativity in that, too. Surely it is the ultimate creative thought to remove oneself from the storm while others are too busy reaping sunshine to notice the dark growth overhead—that cloud of what I've learned, my superstitions, falseness, failure, and even the successes masquerading as something more ominous, the cloud that no one who lives, escapes.

Yet, what is the deception here? Nietzsche tells us there is one, that the rational man "executes his masterpiece of deception in misfortune." What then is the deception? The unchangeable human face—the stoic? The slowness of his steps—logic? The very idea that you can walk from beneath the cloud (philosophy)—or even walk at all (religion)? Misfortune itself?

Wherever the deception lies, the fact that the rational man deceives and makes art, a masterpiece, of his deception proves that the rational man can know the truth he seeks, but he can choose to shroud it, to operate on opposite terms, to bring others in on his deliberate preference for the denial of truth.

If this is so, and if the head of Nietzsche's rational man is what's rearing inside of me, a writer I cannot be, for, as I'm constantly told, "A good poet [writer, creator] is someone who manages, in a lifetime of standing out in thunderstorms, to be struck by lightning five or six times; a dozen or two dozen times and he is great" (Randall Jarrell). The rational man removes himself from such a storm and would thus avoid this brand of greatness, yet what human creates in order to not achieve some sort of greatness? And if the storm itself is a deception, then what strikes the writer but lies? And if, as Plato says, "poetry is nearer to vital truth than history," how could the rational man, usually "seek[ing] nothing but [...] truth" yet creating "masterpiece[s] of deception" ignore the creative force of poetry, or of writing?

That would, then, make creativity the great deception rather than misfortune. It would make the writer the most conflicted of all creatures—truth seeker, truth bearer; professional liar, deception weaver. Perhaps the rational man and the intuitive man are two extremes. Or perhaps they are the Nietzschean equivalent to the id and the ego, being, rather than two separate men, two forces constantly at play in one man. Truthful and deceptive, both, but in opposite arenas. Perhaps from this flux, from this constant conflict, from the overlap, is where creativity is born and truth is found. For, as Yeats, a product of Nietzsche's influence, wrote, "out of the quarrel with ourselves we make poetry"; out of this internal conflict springs forth products of creativity, products of vital truth. And that is what the writer seeks—or, at least, feigns to seek.

Yet, in the ebb and flow, one of these two people, intuitive man and rational man, must at times override, and if I'm to be a scholar, surely it must be the rational man to prevail. That was what Nietzsche was arguing, was it not? In the favor of the rational man and against the silly whims to which the intuitive man was a slave?

And this is when I realized two things: first, that I am the rational man. And second, that the great deception of which Nietzsche writes is the rational man. Which means I am the

Chapter Five

deception.

I reviewed my intellectual pursuits in light of this. Philosophy, that grand deception of wisdom, wherein I could examine a hundred possible truths without ever actually claiming a single truth because everything can be hedged behind the phrase, "to play devil's advocate [...]." Perhaps if I had listened, I would have noted a whisper of desire to feel passionate about one of these truths, but such a thing would have been irrational. Literature, that grand deception of the speculative, wherein I could explicate any sentence of any story and fabricate some meaning out of it worthy of an A- research paper. Perhaps if I had not spent so much time concerned with duality (is that experience positive or negative? Is that decision right or wrong? Is my thesis correct or incorrect?), I would have realized that I had made fiction of myself rather than ever recognize or tell my story. Religion, that grand deception of faith, wherein I could prosthelytize convincingly or mark myself the greatest skeptic for a day or two if only I was well-versed enough in certain tenants. Perhaps if I'd noticed the hunger gnawing in myself for something to believe in, I wouldn't have been trapped by a devil for so long. Poetry, that grand deception of beauty, wherein I could lay in beds of sensual imagery and pleasant-sounding rhythm while I waited to hear indicators of form. Perhaps if I had paused, I would have seen flashing by the beauty of the real world 'round me as I rushed to classes on Transcendentalism.

Because for years, I studied the philosophy of the rational man, sacrificed at the altar of the rational man, molded my life into a story driven by the main character, Rational Man, thought of the rational man as the most beautiful and desirable person on the planet. I struggled to humanize essays and arguments, to make them personal. I was too cold, people said. My works, though "well-written" and "thoughtful" had no feeling. They could not echo. And for years, I tried to mask this rational man in me with the face of the intuitive man in order to be more accessible. But I don't think many believed my deception; and when I look in the mirror, I see that the rational man was a deception in himself, a mask I'd put on the moment I stepped foot in the college classroom and began to understand what the true cost of a diploma was.

Creativity restored. Intuitive man reigns happily ever after. My essential self regained and purified. That's where my story should end, sentimentally?

But the Tin Man didn't get a heart the moment he realized he was without one. Emotion could not return to me simply because the veil was lifted. I needed to understand when the rational man had become my idol in order to understand where I had abandoned all feeling, the capacity to trip over and over again as I harvested the "illumination, cheer, and redemption" to all the glorious irrationalities that come with barricading myself against misfortune.

I thought this part, finding a moment in time, would be exceedingly difficult. It wasn't. I remember that single day on a calendar easily. I don't know if it was the first time the rational man was paraded before me, but it was certainly when the intuitive man was frightened right out of me. My first creative writing class, my fourth or fifth time to workshop my own writing with my peers. I wrote a personal memoir chronicling my experience of losing a close friend to suicide. The grief, the numbness, the anger, the funeral, the burial, the months after. Scene after scene of imagery, thought, and feeling. The actual events had occurred over a year before the workshop, and though I knew the process of revision could be difficult for me given the topic, I felt prepared for that. Enough time had elapsed. The topic was a good one; I wrote from a place of the heart, and yet I structured it well. Tightly knit. Cohesive. Grammatically impeccable. Not perfect, not at all, but I knew it was good enough to avoid steep criticism and encourage insightful, constructive criticism.

The overwhelming response from both my classmates and peers reinforced these things that I already knew. But on all counts, they decried the memoir as lacking something, as failing in some way. It was illogical, they said. They couldn't

Chapter Five

understand *why* my friend killed himself, they said. It was irrational. The whole essay was nonsensical without understanding the *reasons*.

I told them I didn't know, and that's why I wrote. Death didn't make sense. That's why I wrote. To try to make sense of things that didn't have reasons.

They could only reiterate that the essay didn't work without explaining my friend's reasons for killing himself. As if I knew. As if I could write my life like fiction and understand the reasons behind things that had no reason.

I received a low grade on the memoir, I received looks of pity from the other writers whose works had been published in the school literary magazine, and I hated the intuitive man. I hated feeling. Nothing good came from it but fear and bad grades and bad writing and the desire to melt into the floor.

Enter the rational man.

Enter those years of academic, rational exploration—fruitless pursuits. The belief that the rational man trumped the intuitive man on every count.

But if the intuitive man was frightened out of me, what then was the rational man but a mask for fear? I, a mimicry of the rational man, was a deception unto myself, masked, ignorant of my own fear because I imagined that I found myself above it. At least the intuitive man feels the fear of the fall each time he trips into the same ditch. At least he is consistent, "as irrational in sorrow as he is in happiness" (1179). At least "he suffers more intensely [… and] even […] more frequently," since he avoids deception—the requirement that reasons must exist—enough to suffer at all.

Yet, who, in all this searching, would want to settle for merely "at least?" Not everyone can "[count] as real only that life which has been disguised as illusion and beauty" (1179).

In short, who could be satisfied with the intuitive man *or* the rational man? Both deceivers and deceived, both living in fear (whether recognized or suppressed), forced to choose between reason and intuition. The dichotomy is so commonplace that no one bats an eye at it: are you right brained or left brained? Do you like social sciences or natural sciences? Are you a solitary learner or a social learner? There are only two choices, two men to be. And I no longer want to live in light of two. I am unsatisfied. For Nietzsche sought what I seek: freedom. And both men—rational and intuitive—are slaves, forever bound to fear as long as they masquerade and march in parades of arrogance and deception or forgetful suffering and bliss.

To be sure, I am aware that I cannot live in the absence of fear. I am aware of my body, and my muscles, no matter my mental and emotional tenacity. My reflexes jerk me away from the stove top when my fingers graze the surface—and on a basic, biological level, that simultaneous fear and desire for survival fuel that response. My mind may will to survive for power, for art, for God—any number of things. But my body pursues existence, and the fibers of my being quite literally fear—not emotionally, but biologically—the end.

And again, both Nietzsche and I are left with the deepest of conundrums. Living in fear is inevitable, and only acceptance of it brings some measure of freedom. I am pursuing the impossible, the paradox. Should I not just give up? Resign myself to yesteryear's rational man syndrome? Try something new and spend my days falling in the same ditch like the rational man?

Maybe the conundrum is not in the options given, but in the questions themselves. Sven Birkerts, in an essay on Nietzsche's distant counterpart, Emerson, writes, "that the world *seems always waiting* seems incontestable, the feeling of waiting is everywhere—it is, I think, what makes us ever more deeply enslaved to our devices [...]. We are waiting for something that will feel like a solution when it arrives; we are waiting for the oppression of 'what's next?' to be lifted" (73). This is the crux of Nietzsche's point in writing the tale of the intuitive

Chapter Five

man and the rational man. It is not merely the rational and intuitive men who are enslaved. Those who wait to solve the puzzle of which man is best, those who wait for an answer, are the enslaved. We ask the wrong questions, and wait for the answers, the "solutions," that not only seem like solutions but *feel* like solutions. And the answers can never come, and so we are always oppressed by the unanswerable "what's next?"

But questions are necessary, are they not? How can we avoid questions? They are in our every day, in the pause after a statement as we wait for a response, in the moment before the pitcher slides from the counter and shatters, in the way a song doesn't resolve, when a poem resounds in our eardrums and we don't even know what words were spoken, only that they moved. That's all poetry, too, but doesn't it all come down to the word? I write to understand, but I must always begin with the question. For me, here, the question I first penned, "what is creativity and where has mine gone?" (though maybe in not so many words), has not been solved but transcended. I don't demand the dissolution of queries; I wish to escape the stagnant ones.

Questions, then, are a given. For the writer, and especially for the essayist, questions are a must; as William Gass points out, "the essay induces skepticism [...]. [It] is simply a watchful form." Perhaps this is my enslavement, then: to duality. To the question begged and rigged. Are you a poet or a prose writer? Is Beowulf the monster or the hero? Do you adhere to the idea of the essential self or the socially constructed self? Are you the rational man or the intuitive man?

Was not this arrogance, categorization, the thing about which Nietzsche was writing about in "On Truth and Lies in a Non-moral Sense?" After all, he states, "I make up the definition of a mammal, and then, after inspecting a camel, declare 'look, a mammal'" (1175). So, I, too, examine Nietzsche's definition of the rational man, inspect myself, and declare, "look, a rational man!" But in doing this, I come closer not to truth, but to arrogance, an existence in which I have only succeeded in "designat[ing] the relations of things to men"—the fruitless parceling of truth and lies that leads to no "adequate expression of all realities" (1173).

Have I no access to the truth through language, then? If that be the case, why did Nietzsche and his intellectual descendants write? We may not understand the tree, but do we even understand ourselves? Or is this not what writing sets out to do? As Gass points out, "now the philosopher, the theologian, takes over from the poet like the Hyde in Jekyll, and wearily works his world out…" (21). We do this work in writing, futile as our metaphors may be. But again, in writing, we seek to divide, to "describe the mechanisms of its perception, its hierarchies of value, the limits of our knowing and unknowing within that image, since he is [we are] at once the owner and surveyor and policeman of the dream" (21). Through what Nietzsche deems the greatest arrogance, language and adherence to the infallibility of our own knowledge, we self-perpetuate the cycle. I write a paper to support one of two possibilities, and a web of metaphors supports my thesis; everything is either argument or counterargument, truth or lie.

And I don't even like gray area. I much prefer certainty. Yes or no, truth or lie, black or white.

But I think back to my friend, to the suicide. His neck broken by a rope. Garage door opened, a father discovering a still-warm body minutes too late. The frantic seconds of hope as the rope is severed until the possibility of life is denied by the confirmation of death. The unexpected phone call the next morning, the funeral, the burial. The fingerprints on the window as I pressed my nose to the glass to catch one last glimpse of a flower-adorned grave I would never return to.

Was he the rational man or the intuitive man? Monster or hero? Right or wrong?

Those were not the questions I asked in the moments of fear and uncertainty that ensued. When my arrogance was stripped away in the aftermath, I did not ask questions of duality, questions with predisposed answers. I did ask "why?"

but that wasn't my reason for writing. I wrote for the "what?" What happened, what he said, what he did, what I felt, what comes next. In the land between, I sought some connection, an understanding. My classmates saw merely the "why," and the details of my "what" were irrelevant to the question they wanted answered. And perhaps I sought the same, but was more fortunate because in unrelenting pursuit, I still managed to spark something beyond a single question regarding my own creativity—which didn't ever really fail me, but like me, was in the process of becoming.

The creative woman executes her attempt at becoming, wearing no mask, but a human face, asymmetrical, and steps into storm and sun to walk and write beneath them.

Works Cited

Birkerts, Sven. "Emerson's 'The Poet'—A Circling." *Poetry Foundation 200.1* (2012): 69-79. Print.

Gass, William H. "Emerson and the Essay." *Habitations of the Word: Essays*. Ithaca, NY: Cornell UP, 1997. 9-47. Print.

Nietzsche, Friedrich. "On Truth and Lies in a Nonmoral Sense." *The Rhetorical Tradition: Readings from Classical Times to the Present*. 2nd ed. Ed. Patricia Bizzell and Bruce Herzberg. New York: Bedford/St. Martin's, 2000. 1171-79. Print.

This piece is remarkable to me because it is such an intense meditation on Nietzsche's work—so much so that, as you can see, academic writing conventions (e.g., the use of traditional citations) fall away, much like one finds in published personal essays. The work seems to be about the exercise, itself—certainly not about conforming to the "rules" of writing, as they are often articulated in writing assignment rubrics. Instead, this is an excellent example of an essay that gets into the ring with Nietzsche's concepts of the intuitive man, the rational man, and his Zarathustra. The writer, Holly, is after inspiration, but she wants to get at that inspiration not just conceptually or "in theory"; rather, she wants to get at it through the intuitive experience of writing the essay, itself.

Perhaps as a consequence, the essay is, admittedly, at times laborious—sometimes unwieldy, sometimes confused—but knowing Holly's work, I know that this, in and of itself, constituted much of the risk. Giving her self and the question over entirely to the writing, to exploring and examining her self and the question, was a task unlike any other she'd taken on in prior (non-self-writing focused) courses. Even in the prior self writing course she completed with me, she did not take the same kinds of risks in her writing; her engagement with the practices of self writing was not as intense and sustained. So, given her relative newness to the practices, the essay is not perfect; it's certainly not an easy read. But, that's part of my point: students, when they are taking great risks like these in self writing, may not write tidy, easy-to-follow, easy-to-interpret essays. I have to do a lot more work, as a reader, in self writing courses because the essays demand much more of me, but that is, to my mind, one of the great benefits to me personally. I am challenged by the readings, as the students are challenged by the writing.

As part of that challenge, Holly is using all of the self writing practices I talked about in Chapter 3—the disparate (i.e., the truth test) and unification. Like Cameron, she starts with a question in order to open up the meditation: why can't she create? In some ways, though, Holly is in a different place from Cameron. She already accepts that she is "drink[ing] constantly of the streams of the greatest creative minds" and that she is, consequently, made by/in that process. Her frustration is that she doesn't know how to "do something" with that making. This difficulty or frustration demonstrates an important point about the practice of unification. Unification is only possible through the practices of meditation—reading and writing—which Holly is clearly already and always participating in as a student; however, to actually make productive the practices of unification, she must "digest" the material she's read and make it her (not her own, but her self), as explained in Chapter 3. She realizes as much later in the essay, when she says that she never allowed herself to become "passionate" in her relation to and work with any of the ideas or texts she talks about in the narrative of her prior training. Her realization suggests a desire for a different level of engagement in meditating on concepts and texts. In short, she realizes that she was learning *about* concepts and texts without learning how to make them do work for/in her.

Clearly, Holly's engagement is different in this essay. She's not just figuring out what Nietzsche's work is about; she's testing out his claims and concepts, applying them to her own life to try to make sense of them (and in turn, to make sense of her self). In particular, she seems to be after a single claim, relentlessly engaging with it throughout her essay: "[the rational man] executes his masterpiece of deception in misfortune." Holly's question about her own creative life, then, deals in two generative foci for meditation: what does it mean for the rational man to execute his masterpiece of deception in misfortune? And, how might that explain her current frustration and inability to create? What she finds is that in staving off the irrevocable nagging/longing that seems to drive her, in trying to meet that nagging/longing's appetite with various Truths, she's created an intellectual life that fails to appease that appetite and that succeeds only in making her a "rational man," a stoic, of sorts—one who is intensely intellectual and [delusionally] not beholden to the damage of longing. Consequently, however, she finds that she's killed off (or silenced) the productive potentiality of that longing—creativity, itself.

It's worth noting that in talking with Holly at different points in the process, she made clear to me that the particular practices of the disparate and of unification were not taken up in each paragraph deliberately/consciously. Other practices were clearly taken up deliberately: e.g., her use of shifting tenses in the second paragraph to suggest that her grappling with the ideas she introduces there had not come to any end, and her placement of Nietzsche's quote at particular points in her essay to frame and create tensions in the work. However, the meditative practices of the disparate and of unification were not (even though, I'm now convinced that, in some ways, Holly's essay is a reflection on the practices themselves—e.g., on the pay-offs for practicing unification). Point being, I think that the lack of "deliberateness" around the self writing practices is due to Holly having had a chance to practice self writing in an extended essay prior to this one (in a personal essay course she took with me the year before). Given her sustained and intense engagement with the practices in the earlier course, I believe that she had already internalized these practices and was able to reach further, take bigger risks, using them on the page in such a way as to produce a productive self-to-self relation. In fact, at the end of the semester, she shared a letter she addressed to Nietzsche in which she talked about how the engagement with his work enabled a self-on-the-page that transformed her. Holly is, quite simply, not the same writer or individual she was when she walked into the course *because of* the essaying, because of the meditative practices of self writing.

A CONCLUSION

To my mind, it is for these experiences that I teach and that I teach the personal essay in particular. I confess that there was a time in my life when I wrote personal essays because readers/teachers told me I was good at them, and I liked the validation. There was a time, too, that I taught them because my students enjoyed the validating effects of writing papers about themselves. However, now, I know that personal essays can do much more than provide an opportunity for students to have their voices and/or their experiences validated. That's not to say that this validation is not important; it is, especially when my often-marginalized students (e.g., those who are of ethnic minorities or who live in poverty) find a self-on-the-page that feels more authentic and empowering to them. That said, as a writing teacher, that's not my only job.

The potential I see in the personal essay and that I see manifest in my students' work (e.g., in Cameron's and Holly's essays) gets right at the heart of what I believe is education's potential. Like any Rhetoric and Composition Ph.D, I have learned the value of diversity, and part of that valuing has meant considerable time and energy, thought and work, devoted to discovering ways of teaching writing that don't simply indoctrinate students into particular conceptions of "the ethical speaker." On the other hand, I've become increasingly uncomfortable with the mantra that "everything is an argument," as well as the attendant assumption that the individual's job is to identify arguments and, then, consciously select which to accept and which to reject. How is simply selecting arguments (or claims), like one selects produce at the grocery store, productive? In our intensely consumerism-driven culture, isn't that practice far too likely to be dictated by one's own preferences and according to one's identity ("I am a vegetarian, so I like broccoli"), instead of by a desire or need for reconciliation, resolution, and/or transformation? How could it possibly enable debate beyond the trappings of "mere spat," as Crowley and Hawhee have called it?

In a recent article in *The New York Times*, Brendan Nyhan (an assistant professor of government at Dartmouth College) writes about a recent study conducted by Yale Law School professor, Dan Kahan, who finds, according to Nyhan, that "with science, as with politics, identity often trumps the facts" (3). In other words, if I identify as a conservative or as a liberal, if I identify as a Christian or an atheist, that identity will win out, when I am faced with facts that may betray or conflict with my own belief system, as a conservative/liberal, Christian/atheist. As a rhetorician, I am deeply invested in the idea that facts are interpretations of information that is, itself, constituted by [discourse-specific] language and formulas for thought. On the other hand, the treatment of all arguments as equal and the belief that one simply can and should select the arguments that one likes or agrees with and reject others are damaging practices that increasingly threaten the productive functioning of this democracy. Obviously, not all arguments are equal (some are more dominant and pervasive than others, for example). Obviously, I cannot simply select what arguments I like and reject others in some belief buffet. Or, perhaps I can, but in order for them to do any real work—on me, on others, on the discourse—choice is not enough. There are whole histories that come with a particular argument (that make the argument make sense) and politics that dictate its value. To ignore both is to rob the argument of its place in those histories and politics, to rob it, in the end, of its ability to be engaged as more than simply a product to be consumed, as more than simply an idea to be adopted to affirm who and what I already think I am.

That said, I recognize that this book is an argument. Of course it is. It must be so. But, that doesn't mean that because I, too, participate in argument in the writing of this book, then argument is inherently productive or more productive than essaying. In fact, I worry that this book and that the argument made in it will prove impotent—not just because of certain failures working in this particular argument, but because it is one of a world of arguments and because readers who identify as, say, voice pedagogues or social constructionists will reject it out of hand for the fundamental differences it forwards regarding the very principles and axioms on which we work, as writing teachers, scholars, and practitioners.

I don't harbor any delusions about what I'm asking in calling for teachers of writing to get beyond argument, to get beyond paper assignments that ask students to "nail down a thesis" and to argue for it by selecting, "reading," and essentially parroting similar claims made in other sources. We are only encouraging the "buffet-style" thinking about arguments and claims that I've discussed above by doing so. No doubt, my call asks for changes to curriculum that start at our most basic conceptions of what we are and what we should be doing when we teach writing. As we currently, typically teach argument, though, how much hope can we have for real debate, for genuine and rigorous negotiation among individuals and communities around the most important issues at work in our world, when our students are learning to write these kinds of arguments—*without* the sustained and rigorous engagement, the relentless meditation on the larger issues at stake in any argument? As cruel as this indictment sounds, I say it with great conviction: we are fools to think that argument will work. We need a different way, a different set of practices.

According to Spellmeyer in *Arts of Living*, if we want to save the Humanities (including creative and academic writing) from irrelevance, then we must become involved, again, in the "making of culture" (7). In order to make culture, he says that we will have to make connections; we will have to move away from the elitism that is integral to the aristocracy-that-is-the-academy. I'd agree. In part, he is referring to the aristocracy of certain forms (e.g., the argument) over others (e.g., the essay). He's also referring to the aristocracy of readings of texts that are so discipline-specific that they are utterly inaccessible to any scholar or student outside of that discipline. Too, though, I think he is referring to the aristocracy of certain kinds of evidence and certain kinds of knowledge-making in the academy—an aristocracy that shuts out any other kind of engagement with ideas, with beliefs, with arguments.

Spellmeyer uses these claims to set up the argument that he has made in many of his works: that it is in the "universal" human experience that we discover connections with our fellow beings. I'd suggest, though, that it is in the variation and differences among us that we can discover connections—connections that are not constituted in sameness but in the infinite variety (in the encounter with the other that is the self, for example), which when brought into a productive relation, enables endless possibilities for exploration and new "knowing." In other words, I think that the poststructuralists who have taught us the power-play of difference and the tyranny of sameness have offered anyone invested in the personal essay an opportunity to articulate, to encourage, and to explore all of the "difference" and the dynamics at work in those differences that many poststructuralist thinkers, the so-called "elitists," have theorized for so many decades now. In short, it is personal essay scholars, practitioners, and teachers who have an opportunity to help to save the Humanities by teaching and enabling productive debate: by sharing and practicing ways of engaging with ideas and beliefs, ways of engaging with individuals and communities that get beyond the failures of argument.

I can't give up on the possibility of a just world—or at least a just writing assignment. I think that essaying can be exactly that. It provides students with the opportunity to engage rigorously with a topic or question and in a sustained (though, perhaps unwieldy) exercise. It teaches them the value of writing-through a question. It does not ask them to answer some enormous question (like whether the death penalty is just or unjust, whether abortion is an issue of the fetus's rights or the mother's, whether stricter gun laws would infringe on our human rights or better protect them, etc.) in a single statement and to forward that thesis concisely and without thoroughly addressing and examining any complications to it. If our students' arguments in our own courses—courses that are supposed to deal explicitly with written articulation and negotiation of ideas and beliefs—have proven to be ultimately impotent in changing the game (the game being written articulation and negotiation inside and outside of our classrooms), then isn't it time to think differently, to be innovative in our thinking around the training of student writers, as both future writers in their disciplines and as citizens?

It is for this possibility—our own, our students', and even the Humanities'—that I offer this book.

NOTES

37. In "Attitudes toward Imitation," Dale Sullivan takes this passage from Quintilian to mean that "[w]ide reading, though not exactly an exercise, is imitative in nature because it is based on the assumption that students will unconsciously assimilate stylistic qualities, rhetorical strategies, and a fund of ideas from great writers" (14). Perhaps Sullivan is correct in his reading of the implicit assumptions at work in this form of imitation; likely, it is the same series of assumptions at work in teaching students the essay by having them read lots of canonized essays. Students are assumed to pick up the insights and strategies of great writers through what looks

like a process of osmosis. As I have shown in Chapter 4, though, imitation can be a meditative practice—one that requires a different kind of engagement.

38. On a related note, by encouraging the practice of reading and writing-in-response to texts, I help my students to avoid the experience of being so overwhelmed with the concepts and movement of a dense text that they "retain nothing" or "forget themselves." Foucault explains: "[W]ithout taking notes or constituting a treasure store of reading—one is liable to retain nothing, to spread oneself across different thoughts, and to forget oneself" ("Self Writing" 211). Here, Foucault is suggesting more than the experience of forgetting what one has read; he's suggesting that in forgetting what one has read, one forgets his/her [constituted] self—the self that has been made in the practice of reading. For this reason and others, the symbiotic practices of reading and writing are absolutely essential to students' success in the course.

WORKS CITED

Anderson, Chris. "Hearsay Evidence and Second-Class Citizenship." *College English* 50.3 (1988): 300-08. Print.
Atkins, G. Douglas. *Estranging the Familiar: Toward a Revitalized Critical Writing*. Athens: U of Georgia P, 1992. Print.
Bartholomae, David. "Response." In "Interchanges: Responses to Bartholomae and Elbow." *College Composition and Communication* 46.1 (1995): 84-87. Print.
—. "Writing with Teachers: A Conversation with Peter Elbow." *College Composition and Communication* 46.1 (1995): 62-71. Print.
Bartholomae, David and Anthony Petrosky. *Ways of Reading: An Anthology for Writers*. 4th ed. Boston: Bedford Books of St. Martin's Press, 1996. Print.
Bensmaïa, Réda. *The Barthes Effect: The Essay as Reflective Text*. Trans. Pat Fedkiew. *Theory and History of Literature* 54 (1987). Print.
Berlin, James. "Rhetoric and Ideology in the Writing Class." *College English* 50.5 (1988): 477-94. Print.
Berry, Wendell. "An Entrance to the Woods." *The Art of the Personal Essay: An Anthology from the Classical Era to the Present*. Ed. Phillip Lopate. New York: Doubleday, 1994. 670-79.
Bishop, Wendy. "Suddenly Sexy: Creative Nonfiction Rear-ends Composition." Creative Nonfiction. Spec. Issue of *College English* 65.3 (2003): 237-322. Print.
Bizzell, Patricia. "Cognition, Convention, and Certainty: What We Need to Know about Writing." *Pre/Text* 3.3 (1982): 213-43. Print.
—. "Foundationalism and Anti-Foundationalism in Composition Studies." *Academic Discourse and Critical Consciousness*. Pittsburgh: U of Pittsburgh P, 1992. 202-21. Print.
—. "What Is a Discourse Community?" *Academic Discourse and Critical Consciousness*. Pittsburgh, PA: University of Pittsburgh Press, 1992. 222-37. Print.
Bloom, Lynn Z. "The Essay Canon." *College English* 61.4 (1999): 401-30. Print.
—. "Living to Tell the Tale: The Complicated Ethics of Creative Nonfiction." Creative Nonfiction. Spec. Issue of *College English* 65.3 (2003): 276-89. Print.
Brodkey, Linda. "Writing on the Bias." *College English* 56.5 (1994): 527-47. Print.
Bryant, Lizbeth. *Voice as Process*. Portsmouth, NH: Boynton Cook, 2005. Print.
Ching, Stuart. "Memory as Travel: The Role of Story in Cultural Resistance and Cultural Change." *Writing on the Edge* 11.2 (2000): 55-67. Print.
Connors, Robert. "The Erasure of the Sentence." *Selected Essays of Robert J. Connors*. New York: Bedford/St. Martins, 2003. 452-78. Print.

Crowley, Sharon, and Debra Hawhee. *Ancient Rhetorics for Contemporary Students*. 5th ed. Boston: Pearson, 2012. Print.

D'Angelo, Frank J. "Imitation and Style." *College Composition and Communication* 24.3 (1973): 283-90. Print.

Didion, Joan. "On Keeping a Notebook." *Slouching Towards Bethlehem*. New York: Noonday, 1990. 131-41.

Difranco, Ani. "I'm No Heroine." *Living in Clip*. Righteous Babe, 1997. CD.

Elbow, Peter. Introduction. *Landmark Essays: On Voice and Writing*. Ed. Peter Elbow. Davis, CA: Hermagoras, 1994. xi-xivii. Print.

—. "Voice in Writing Again: Embracing Contraries." *College English* 70.2 (2007): 168-88. Print.

—. *Writing Without Teachers*. New York: Oxford UP, 1973. Print.

—. *Writing With Power: Techniques for Mastering the Writing Process*. New York: Oxford UP, 1981. Print.

Emerson, Ralph Waldo. "Nature." *The Best of Ralph Waldo Emerson: Essays, Poems, Addresses*. Roslyn, NY: Walter J. Black, Inc. 1941. 73-116. Print.

Faigley, Lester. *Fragments of Rationality: Postmodernity and the Subject of Composition*. Pittsburgh: U of Pittsburgh P, 1992. Print.

Foucault, Michel. *Care of the Self: Vol. 3 of History of Sexuality*. Trans. Robert Hurley. New York: Vintage, 1988. Print.

—. "The Ethics of the Concern for Self as a Practice of Freedom." *Ethics, Subjectivity and Truth: The Essential Works of Michel Foucault, 1954-1984*. Vol. 1. Ed. Paul Rabinow. Trans. Robert Hurley and Others. New York: New Press, 1997. 281-301. Print.

—. "An Historian of Culture." *Foucault Live: Interviews, 1961-1984*. Ed. By Sylvere Lotringer. Trans. Lysa Hochroth and John Johnston. New York: Semiotext(e), 1989. 95-104. Print.

Foucault, Michel, Luther H. Martin, Huck Gutman, and Patrick H. Hutton. *Technologies of the Self: A Seminar with Michel Foucault*. Amherst: U of Massachusetts P, 1988. 16-49. Print.

Foucault, Michel. "Self Writing." *Ethics, Subjectivity and Truth: The Essential Works of Michel Foucault, 1954-1984*. Vol. 1. Ed. Paul Rabinow. Trans. Robert Hurley and Others. New York: New Press, 1997. 207-22. Print.

—. "What is an Author?" *Aesthetics, Method, and Epistemology: The Essential Works of Michel Foucault, 1954-1984*. Vol. 2. Ed. James D. Faubion. Trans. Robert Hurley and Others. New York: New Press, 1998. 205-22. Print.

Gass, William H. "Emerson and the Essay." *Habitations of the Word: Essays*. New York: Simon, 1985. 9-49. Print.

Good, Graham. *The Observing Self: Rediscovering the Essay*. New York: Routledge, 1988. Print.

Gonzales, Lawrence. "Marion Prison." *Creating Nonfiction: A Guide and Anthology*. Ed. Becky Bradway and Doug Hesse. New York: Bedford/St. Martin's, 2009. 403-27. Print.

Greene, Liz, and Juliet Sharman-Burke. *The Mythic Tarot*. Chagrin Falls, OH: Fireside, 1986. Print.

Gruber, William. "Servile Copying' and the Teaching of English Composition." *College English* 39.4 (1977): 491-97. Print.

Gusdorf, Georges. "Scripture of the Self: 'Prologue in Heaven.'" *Studies in Autobiography*. Ed. James Olney. New York: Oxford UP, 1988. 112-27. Print.

—. *Speaking (La Parole)*. Evanston, IL: Northwestern UP, 1965. Print.

Hall, Michael. "The Emergence of the Essay and the Idea of Discovery." *Essays on the Essay: Redefining the Genre*. Ed. Alexander Butrym. Athens: U of Georgia P, 1989. 73-91. Print.

Harris, Jeanette. "Constructing and Reconstructing the Self in the Writing Class." *Journal of Teaching Writing* 8.1 (1989): 21-29.

Harris, Joseph. "Community: A Keyword in the Teaching of Writing." Paper presented at: Annual Meeting of the Conference on College Composition and Communication. St. Louis: Mar. 1988. *ERIC*. Web. 20 August 2012.

—. *A Teaching Subject: Composition Since 1966*. Upper Saddle River, NJ: Prentice, 1997. Print.

Hazlitt, William. "On Going a Journey." *The Art of the Personal Essay: An Anthology from the Classical Era to the Present*. Ed. Phillip Lopate. New York: Doubleday, 1994. 181-89. Print.

Heilker, Paul. *The Essay: Theory and Pedagogy for an Active Form*. Urbana, IL: NCTE, 1996.

Heitsch, Dorothea B. "Nietzsche and Montaigne: Concepts of Style." *Rhetorica: A Journal of the History of Rhetoric* 17.4 (1999): 411-31. Print.

hooks, bell. "When I Was a Young Soldier for the Revolution: Coming to Voice." *Landmark Essays: On Voice and Writing*. Ed. Peter Elbow. Davis, CA: Hermagoras, 1994. 51-58. Print.

Ivins, Molly. "Texas Women: True Grit and All the Best." *Shadow Boxing: Art and Craft in Creative Nonfiction*. Ed. Kristen Iversen. Upper Saddle River, NJ: Pearson/Prentice Hall, 2004. 52-56. Print.

Jarratt, Susan. *Rereading the Sophists: Classical Rhetoric Refigured*. Carbondale: Southern Illinois UP, 1991. Print.

Kingsolver, Barbara. "Household Words." *Small Wonder: Essays*. New York: HarperCollins, 2002. 195-205. Print.

Knoeller, Christian. *Voicing Ourselves: Whose Words We Use When We Talk About Books*. New York: SUNY P, 1998. Print.

Leonard, Elisabeth Anne. "Assignment #9: A Text Which Engages the Socially

Constructed Identity of Its Writer." *College Composition and Communication* 48.2 (1997): 215-30. Print.

Longinus. *On the Sublime. Classical Literary Criticism.* Translation and introduction by T. S. Dorsch. New York: Penguin, 1965. 99-158. Print.

Lopate, Phillip. Introduction. *The Art of the Personal Essay: An Anthology from the Classical Era to the Present.* New York: Doubleday, 1994. xxiii-liv. Print.

Lukács, Georg. *Soul and Form.* Trans. Anna Bostock. London: Merlin, 1974. Print.

Martinez, Demetria. "Inherit the Earth" and "The Things They Carried." *Creating Nonfiction: A Guide and Anthology.* Ed. Becky Bradway and Douglas D. Hesse. Boston: Bedford/St. Martin's, 2009. 567-70. Print.

Miller, Richard E. "Fault Lines in the Contact Zones." *College English* 56.4 (1994): 389-408. Print.

Miller, Susan. *Rescuing the Subject: A Critical Introduction to Rhetoric and the Writer.* Carbondale: Southern Illinois UP, 1989. Print.

Moffett, James. *Teaching the Universe of Discourse.* Boston: Houghton, 1968. Print.

Montaigne, Michel. *The Complete Essays of Montaigne.* Trans. Donald Frame. Stanford, CA: Stanford UP, 1958. Print.

—. "Of Books." From *The Complete Essays of Montaigne.* 296-305.

—. "Of Experience." From *The Complete Essays of Montaigne.* 815-57.

—. "Of Giving the Lie." From *The Complete Essays of Montaigne.* 503-06.

—. "Of Pedantry." From *The Complete Essays of Montaigne.* 97-106.

—. "Of Presumption." From *The Complete Essays of Montaigne.* 478-502.

—. "Our Feelings Reach Out Beyond Us." From *The Complete Essays of Montaigne.* 8-13.

—. To the Reader. From *The Complete Essays of Montaigne.* 2.

Muckelbauer, John. *The Future of Invention: Rhetoric, Postmodernism, and the Problem of Change.* Albany, NY: SUNY P, 2008.

Nietzsche, Friederich. "On Truth and Lies in a Nonmoral Sense." *The Rhetorical Tradition: Readings from Classical Times to the Present.* 2nd ed. Ed. Patricia Bizzell and Bruce Herzberg. New York: Bedford/St. Martin's, 2000. 1171-79. Print.

—. *On the Genealogy of Morals.* Trans. Walter Kaufmann and RJ Hollingdale. New York: Vintage, 1967. Print.

Nyhan, Brendan. "When Beliefs and Facts Collide." *New York Times* 6 July 2014, The Upshot sec.: 3. Print.

Plato. *Phaedrus and the Seventh and Eighth Letters.* Trans. Walter Hamilton. New York: Penguin, 1973. Print.

Pratt, Mary Louise. "Arts of the Contact Zone." *Profession* 91 (1991): 33-40.

—. "Interpretive Strategies/Strategic Interpretations: On Anglo-American Reader Response Criticism." *Boundary* 2.11 (1982-83): 201-31. Print.

Quintilian. *Quintilian on the Teaching of Speaking and Writing: Translations from Books One, Two, and Ten of the Institutio Oratoria*. Ed. James J. Murphy. Carbondale, IL: Southern Illinois UP, 1987. Print.

Rabinow, Paul. "Introduction: The History of Systems of Thought." In *Ethics, Subjectivity and Truth: Essential works of Michel Foucault, 1954-1984*. Trans. Michael J. Hurley. New York: New York Press, 1997. xi-xlii. Print.

Ramage, John D., John C. Bean, and June Johnson. *The Allyn and Bacon Guide to Writing*. 3rd edition. New York: Longman, 2003. Print.

Robertson, Elizabeth, and Bruce Martin. "Culture as Catalyst and Constraint: Toward a New Perspective on Difference." *College English* 62.4 (2000): 492-510. Print.

Rohmann, Gordon, and Albert Wlecke. "Pre-Writing: The Construction and Application of Models for Concept Formation in Writing." U.S. Department of Health, Education, and Welfare Cooperative Research Project No. 2174. East Lansing: Michigan State University, 1964. Print.

Root, Robert, and Michael Steinberg. Introduction. *The Fourth Genre: Contemporary Writers of/on Creative Nonfiction*. 2nd ed. New York: Longman, 2002. xxiii-xxxiii. Print.

Sanders, Scott Russell. "The Singular First Person." *Secrets of the Universe: Scenes from the Journey Home*. Boston: Beacon, 1991.187-204. Print.

Seneca. "On Gathering Ideas." *Epistles 66-92*. Trans. Richard M. Gummere. Cambridge, MA: Harvard University Press, 2006. 276-85. Print.

Spellmeyer, Kurt. "A Common Ground: The Essay in the Academy." *College English* 51.3 (1989): 262-76. Print.

—. *Arts of Living: Reinventing the Humanities for the Twenty-First Century*. Albany, NY: SUNY P, 2003. Print.

Stoehr, Taylor. "Tone and Voice." *College English* 30.2 (1968): 150-61. Print.

Strange, G. Robert. "The Voices of the Essayist." George Eliot. Spec. Issue of *Nineteenth-Century Fiction* 35.3 (1980): 312-30. Print.

Sullivan, Dale. "Attitudes toward Imitation: Classical Culture and the Modern Temper." *Rhetoric Review* 8.1 (1989): 5-21. Print.

Veyne, Paul. "Foucault Revolutionizes History." In *Foucault and His Interlocuters*. Trans. Catherine Porter. Ed. Arnold I. Davidson. Chicago: U of Chicago P, 1978. 146-82. Print.

Wordsworth, William. "Composed A Few Miles Above Tintern Abbey, On Revisiting The Banks Of The Wye During A Tour. July 13, 1798." *The Complete Poetical Works*. London: Macmillan and Co., 1888; Bartleby.com, 1999. Web. <http://www.bartleby.com/145/ww138.html>.

ABOUT THE AUTHOR

Sarah Allen is an Associate Professor in the English Department at the University of Northern Colorado in Greeley, Colorado, where she serves as a Rhetoric and Composition scholar and teacher. Her work has been published in *Rhetoric Review* and in *Educational Philosophy and Theory*; she also has book chapters in *Writing Spaces: Readings on Writing* (Parlor Press) and in *Research Writing Revisited: A Sourcebook for Teachers* (Heinemann). Her scholarship generally explores the ethics of the personal essay, and this work informs her teaching, as she works to discover the most useful and effective ways of assisting students in engaging with difficult, dense material and in generating complex, rigorous writings of their own.

www.ingramcontent.com/pod-product-compliance
Lightning Source LLC
Chambersburg PA
CBHW020233170426
43201CB00007B/416